CAST A CLEVER LINE

Angling missions for species and specimens

John Martin

The Lissanisk Press

John Martin

First published in 2007 by the Lissanisk Press, The Martin's Nest, 9, Gravel Pits Close, Bredon, Gloucestershire, GL20 7QL (Telephone: 01684 772970, e-mail: themartinsnest@hotmail.com)

© John Martin 2007

ISBN: 0-9548780-1-9

British Library Cataloguing in Publication Data

A catalogue record for this book is available from the British Library

Printing: Alden Group Limited (Witney)

Binding: Green Street Bindery (Oxford)

Cover Design: Eric Holloway, Typecraft (Cheltenham) Ltd

This book is dedicated to my wife, Tricia who has endured my incessant appetite to fish for all these years...

Contents   *Page Number*

Acknowledgements

Having already met all the obstacles of self-publishing when producing my previous book, the journey for this one was always going to be somewhat smoother but nevertheless I could not have done it without a little help from my friends. I would therefore like to extend my gratitude once again to Gill Bradley who was instrumental in putting the finishing touches to my work. Gill, who became known as 'The Oracle', spent many hours searching for grammatical deficiencies and punctuating the draft text, which generally enhanced the flow and readability of the book. Her valued input was such that the book may not have gone to print without it and I shall be eternally grateful to her for helping me to fulfil another dream.

A special thank you goes to my fishing buddies, Rawson Bradley, Richard Fobbester and Dave Minchew who gave up their time to accompany me on a variety of missions for some of the more obscure targets that they had little interest in themselves. I would also like to mention Sam and Gary Edmonds who shared some of their own experiences of tracking down some British rarities, which in turn has helped me to achieve some of my own goals.

With regard to the new technology applications, I owe a great deal to Justin Taylor of the Alden Group and also to my son and daughter, Lee and Sian, who put in a great deal of time and effort on those technical issues.

Finally, my appreciation also goes to the very talented Richard Lott for his caricature, which was created from his own interpretation of the 'Special Catch' taken on the River Severn and to Nicci Booth for her Char fishing illustration.

Introduction

It has been apparent from the positive and complimentary response I received from the readership of my previous book, 'It Started with a Perch', that there are many other anglers out there who, like myself, enjoy chasing a personal best or catching a new species. This, therefore, became my primary reason for deciding to continue the theme with my next offering. I hope this new book will appeal to what I perceive to be a growing band of enthusiasts who are prepared to travel long distances to achieve their objectives. Much of the fun is in the chase, and for success in angling, as in all walks of life, one has to invest heavily in good preparation. I believe it is important to glean as much information as possible about target fish, venues, contacts and methods as an on-going process. Building up a wealth of information in advance from press cuttings and anglers 'in the know' means only the minimum amount of precious time is lost when it comes to arranging a trip. My own records, which are segregated by each target species, are chock full of data enabling me to act without delay in order to achieve a specific goal at the optimum time.

Most of my fishing time during latter years has been spent mainly on Barbel and particularly on the River Severn. I have become absorbed entirely, and apart from when I am on special missions for other species, I try to spend every spare moment on the waters below the City of Worcester. In the main my exploits have been for freshwater fish from lakes and rivers but increasingly, I have been drawn to seeking different species in the sea. Having said this, given an equal chance of catching a new sea or freshwater species, I would take the freshwater option every time. To put my fishing into perspective, I would say that I spend 80% of my time hunting for specimens and 20% hunting species. I have found that fishing a diversity of methods like casting a fly, long trotting or fishing over deep water shipwrecks is not only more satisfying but helps to develop one's all round angling skills which, in many cases, seem to be on the wane these days.

This book highlights a cross section of actual experiences in the search for a variety of different species and specimens, both here in the UK and overseas. As the events portrayed have taken place in a relatively short space of time, the reader will get a perspective of the author's typical angling schedule. He will also find a realistic balance of success stories as well as those of disappointment, showing the true nature of fishing, which, as we know, does not always go according to plan.

Chapter I

Chalk Stream Magic (22.01.2005)

I always try to arrange at least one winter trip each year to fish for Grayling in one of the prestigious chalk streams that grace the south of England. My favourites are the Wylye, Test and Itchen and on this occasion we had chosen the Test. I believe this is the longest river in Hampshire, stretching for about 40 miles. It rises at a place called Ashe, which is near to Overton and flows through Stockbridge and Romsey before emptying into Southampton Water. Dave Minchew and I had booked a day session at Timsbury Manor where there are three miles of bank to explore. The estate provides day tickets, currently at £15, which are only available to a limited number of anglers booking in advance for a few weeks during the Trout and Salmon closed season. My feeling is that anglers who take advantage of this golden opportunity to fish any method are very privileged indeed. This famous chalk stream and its carriers are normally reserved for the fortunate game fishermen who are willing to pay a premium price for the honour. In my view the day tickets are certainly worth every penny...

Rain had fallen continuously for two days prior to our impending visit and we were concerned about the effects it would have on the waters at our chosen locality. To clarify the situation I telephoned the River Keeper the night before we were due to make the trip and was informed that, whilst the river was running just above normal levels with a slight hint of colour, the fishing prospects remained good. With our spirits restored we arranged an early start so as to arrive just before the fishery opened. The 100-mile journey was made without incident, apart from having to avoid some localised flooding in the Marlborough area. In fact we even had time to grab a bite to eat and a cup of coffee in Stockbridge before making our way to the fishery itself. This was my second visit to this venue so I already knew the ropes and was able to set off to fish without having to be shown the footpaths and boundaries. The weather forecast, which can be a bit of a lottery at this time of the year, was light westerly winds and isolated showers. On the day however there was sleet and snow in the air and the temperature was only a degree above freezing - atmospheric pressure was on the low side. That said, the Grayling fishing would be unaffected by the low temperatures and it was only the comfort factor that was of any interest. We had already decided to try our luck in the deeper waters at the farthest point of the fishery first before gradually fishing our way back to the little weir pool next to the car park. The adrenalin was now in full flow, sparked off by the satisfying sound of water surging across the fast riffles of the streams that we were following through the woodlands. Crossing the little bridge over the stream we entered the picturesque water meadow that gave us our first glimpse of the River Test meandering gracefully through the countryside. With a backdrop of deciduous trees, the scene was typical of old England and certainly one to savour - lovely! My instinct was to stop and cast at every mouth-watering beat but discipline was maintained and after about 20 minutes we arrived at the downstream boundary point. The water here was dark and certainly much deeper than the hot-spots we had by-passed earlier. It looked to me to be the perfect place for big Roach, Chub and even perhaps a Salmon and I couldn't wait to send my two swan Drennan loafer float through the glides. My trusty old "Rapidex" pin worked admirably as it allowed the float to travel on its way unhindered. It became hard work though, holding the rod high and continually "mending" the line. Maintaining a direct contact with the float by keeping as much line off the water as possible is sound policy because it avoids drag and helps presentation and striking. As it happened however, the hard work with the rod was in vain because despite continuous feeding and running the float through the near - side, far-side and the middle of the river, I could not buy a bite as they say. Dave, who tried alternative baits such as bread flake and worms, also failed to get a sniff of a fish either. It was time for a move, so after an hour and a half we decided to try elsewhere.

As we made our way upstream, leap-frogging each other to cast in each likely spot, the water became shallower and the Grayling started to come to the net. It was great sport catching fish from about two ounces up to a pound but the bigger fish were proving to be evasive. One frustrating factor was that despite striking at the first indication, most of the Grayling had swallowed the bait and a lot of time was spent trying to disgorge the hook carefully so as not to harm the fish. It was also noticeable that the flow of the river was a lot heavier than I had experienced on the first occasion. Typically something had to ruin the fun – while trying to retrieve my float tackle from a bush after a missed strike, I stepped back on the mid - section of my rod, which promptly shattered. The Drennan Team England special won in a competition was my pride and joy and I was gutted. However, for the sake of not wasting precious time, I had to quickly put the misfortune behind me and get on with the fishing. It was over to my other rod, a light quiver, which had been set up with a small feeder on a running rig. The first job was to shorten the hook link considerably to a matter of inches in order to try to prevent the deep hooking of the Grayling. In the meantime I had made my way back to one of my favourite beats next to the pylon where I intended to remain for a while, so I made myself comfortable. After several minutes of continually drip-feeding maggots via the feeder, the bites started to materialise but I was unable to connect with anything over a pound. I decided to change the bait to a single grain of sweetcorn and my luck changed immediately. My rod folded around as a bigger Grayling weaved and squirmed in the heavy flow, using its flanks and large dorsal fin to good effect to evade capture. Fortunately the hook held firm and I was able to net the fish, which weighed 1lb 11ozs - that was better!

The next stop was where a powerful carrier stream came to join the main river at right angles. The converging flows created an eddying effect on the near-side, next to a large tree growing out of the riverbank. There was only a tiny gap to place a rod just above the point where the roots of the tree disappeared into a deep pool. The place screamed fish and I wondered why I had missed it on my first visit but quickly concluded that it was because the gap between carrier stream and tree was only a matter of inches wide. I put in a couple of handfuls of maggots, which sank into the depths out of vision, before following the bait trail with my feeder and a single maggot on the hook. Placing the quiver rod down and tightening the line, I decided to pour a drink from my flask. Before I had time to wet my lips, I caught a glimpse of the tip of my rod bending beneath the surface of the river as a fish tried to make its escape. I grabbed the rod and the reel immediately started to concede line rapidly. The fish was fighting very aggressively and I thought the line was going to part company at any moment. It was a spirited fish and whilst I had a 3lb breaking strain main line, the hook link was only 2.2lb. I was struggling to cope in the confined space as the fish created havoc downstream behind the tree. It was bolting, boring and jumping all over the place and all I could do was try and keep up the pressure on a tight line. To my relief, after a few minutes of just trying to stay connected, the fish began to tire and the battle became a slower affair. Soon I had regained the line that had been lost and the fish was flashing in the deep pool under the rod tip. Keeping up the pressure, the fish came to the surface where fortunately I was able to net it on the first attempt. I felt sure that it was a Sea Trout because there were sea lice attached to its flanks, but not having seen one before I couldn't be certain. During the fight, the fish had rolled itself up in the line and in fact there were seven complete circles of line coiled around its body when I landed it. In all my fishing years I hadn't encountered this behaviour before and surmised that it was a trait of game-fish of which my angling experiences have been limited. I whistled to Dave who was fishing about 100 yards away, and beckoned him to come and take a look and help with a photograph or two. The fish had fought courageously and I was eager to return it safely to the river as soon as possible. During the weighing process we were joined by the Landlord who apparently had been observing my battle with the fish from the copse behind. He confirmed that my fish was in fact a Sea Trout and that in his opinion the flesh was better eating than that of a Salmon. Before he had time to suggest knocking it on the head, I quickly slipped it back into the river - there was no way that I was going to kill such a beautiful specimen. The scales had registered 4lb 4ozs and I was informed that there were a lot bigger fish to be had and the timing couldn't be better as there were a good number of fish running at that moment. I'm glad to have had the opportunity to talk to the Landlord who was a real down-to-earth, friendly gentleman. He was genuinely interested in how we had fared and made sure our visit was problem-free before continuing on his way. The capture of this fine fish in some way helped me to accept the unfortunate loss of my beloved rod - had I still been using float tackle I'm convinced that I would have by-passed the corner swim and missed out on catching my new personal best. Thank Heavens for small mercies.

I carried on fishing in the little pool by the tree for another hour or so until the bites dried up completely. During that time I managed to bank two more Sea Trout and a Rainbow, which between them averaged about 2½lbs in weight. Meanwhile Dave had put together a significant catch of Grayling and a single Sea Trout that was nudging 4lbs. The skies were now darkening so we decided to make our way back to the small weir pool at the start of the fishery for a final cast.   This little gem of a pool has produced some super Roach, many of which have exceeded the 2lb barrier, and the best time to try for them is dusk when they seem to be more active.   Unfortunately we only had about 15 minutes to fish at the pool before darkness fell and we would have to make our departure.   The River Keeper was waiting for us as we arrived at the pool and by the time we had finished chatting there was very little time left to fish. In fact Dave didn't take the trouble to cast but I couldn't resist plopping my feeder into the flow, where it settled within a foot of the bank. Almost immediately the tip pulled around and after a spirited fight I netted a fourth Sea Trout, which was a couple of pounds or so. The River Keeper pointed out the position of the jaw that reached back beyond the eye, the lice and the dark smudge-like blotches, which are apparently the characteristics to look for when identifying these fish. Anyway, time had run out and I didn't have the opportunity to exploit the Roach potential but it did give me the incentive to make a return visit.   Next time I shall definitely spend at least half a day trying to winkle out one of those big Redfins from the area around the little weir pool.

Chapter II

Lough Neagh (02.08.2005)

One of my burning ambitions is to catch a Whitefish. Whitefish actually cover a range of sub species including Houting, Powan, Gwyniad (also known as Schelly), Vendace and Pollan. I would settle for catching any one of these rare fish but unfortunately they are very difficult to track down in their large deep-water habitats. Whitefish are in fact members of the Salmon family and, as with all Salmonoids, the adipose fin can be found positioned between the dorsal and caudal fins. It would certainly help matters if I could seek advice from an expert but regrettably there are only a handful of anglers who have been lucky enough to have encountered these fish. My previous attempts to locate them in the lakes and mountain tarns of Cumbria have all been in vain and in fact it was like trying to find the proverbial needle in the haystack. Despite the extent of these lakes, which can sometimes stretch for miles, the access and bank space available to fish is normally very limited. Indeed, when I have been able to find a suitable spot to fish, the cast has been made into open, featureless water that is inevitably more than a 100 feet deep directly under the rod tip. Hardly an ideal situation and I soon realised that I had little chance of success and needed to change my approach.

My initial thoughts turned towards Scotland and in particular Loch Lomond where the Powan exists. However I had no idea of the numbers of these fish present and was concerned that I hadn't heard of any catches whatsoever. In fact I wasn't even sure if anyone actually fishes for them there. Needless to say, after dismissing this option and racking my brains further, an idea came to mind that required some additional investigation. Among the variety of pre-packed dead baits now available to Pike anglers is the Pollan, which is netted commercially in Lough Neagh, Northern Ireland. I concluded that these fish must be present in sufficient numbers to make netting a viable proposition and felt that this might be the opportunity I had been looking for. Inspired at last, I decided to write to the Government Department in Belfast to ascertain if fishing for Pollan was in the bounds of possibility. The reply I received from the Senior Fisheries Officer was extremely helpful and encouraging. It transpired that plenty of Pollan are caught in Lough Neagh by fly anglers and the optimum time for catching them is April and May, the favourite choice of fly pattern being the Black Gnat and the Duck Fly. The letter went on to point out that the Lough was also known for a fish named the Dollaghan Trout and that the pleasure angling was a well kept secret! I was also offered help if I was interested in catching other native Trout species including the Sonaghan, Gillaroo and the Ferox. At that stage I felt it may have been a fish too far but I kept the details on file pending further research at a later date. The best bit I've left till last - they had been in touch with a local boatman and keen angler, Alan Kirkpatrick, and obtained his permission for me to contact him. Great news - I lost no time and telephoned him immediately to make some plans. We decided on a four-day visit in August, which was the only time my fishing buddy, Rawson Bradley, and I had available due to work and other commitments. However, in order to maximise the fishing time we thought it was best to travel by air although this would restrict the amount of tackle we could take. Alan didn't envisage any problems with this arrangement and just in case, promised to bring along his fly rod together with a gallon of maggots!

When the big day arrived, both of us stuffed our clothing with items of tackle, and these were tucked away in every nook and cranny ready for the flight across the Irish Sea. I don't know whether it's my outward demeanour or pure bad luck but I was picked out for interrogation as we passed through security at Birmingham Airport. This situation seems to have become customary these days and it's got to the stage when I think something has gone wrong if I don't get stopped on my way through. I remember looking up from my prone position at Rawson who was finding it difficult to hold back his amusement at my predicament. With an officer on each arm, I was suspended just above the floor while a third man checked the bottom of my shoes for hidden explosives - blimey what an embarrassment! Anyway, alls well that ends well and it wasn't too long before I was cleared for take-off for the short flight...

At Belfast International we picked up the hire car and made the relatively short journey to our accommodation in Dunadry where we had arranged to meet Alan. The guesthouse was immaculate and, like most of the rural properties in the region, set in expansive grounds. Alan turned up as planned and after the introductions we got down to sorting out the finer details and more importantly where the boat was to be launched the following morning. On the negative side it was worrying to be informed that the abnormally sultry weather that they had been experiencing for the past few weeks was due to change for the worse. This was just our luck and we would have to keep our fingers crossed that the trip could go ahead.

Next day saw us up with the lark for an early breakfast after which we made the four-mile journey to the quayside at the Marina car park in Antrim to meet Alan. We reached our destination early as usual but my jaw dropped at the sight that stood before us. The Lough had been whipped into a frenzy by a strong wind and the waves were crashing against the rocky margins, sending up clouds of spray along the shoreline. I was dumbfounded by the sheer enormity of the Lough and this, coupled with the picture of turmoil, dampened our spirits somewhat. It was like looking across the sea towards the horizon that seemingly had no end —

a truly awesome spectacle. White horses topped the waves as far as the eye could see and no other boats had visibly braved the rough conditions. On the face of things it seemed a daunting prospect to venture into the great expanse of water to find the Pollan. When Alan arrived he was dismayed and frustrated by the situation but felt that we might have a chance fishing in the lee of Shanes Castle lying on the north-eastern shore of Lough Neagh. We could have taken the decision to postpone for a day or two but the forecast was no better so it would have served no purpose. Our only chance was to give it a try, so the high-powered Orkney Pilot boat was unhitched from the Landrover and between us we managed a successful launch.

As we motored out Alan gave us a bit of background information about Lough Neagh. The Lough, which is the biggest freshwater lake in the British Isles, covers about 150 square miles. It is 18 miles long and 11 miles wide and it's shores touch five of the six counties of Northern Ireland. I think that just about puts the place into perspective. Irish Mythology has it that Lough Neagh was the result of an argument between two Giants. It is said that Finn MacCool, who was supposed to have built the Devil's Causeway, scooped up a sod of earth to hurl at his rival, a Scottish Giant named Fingal. His aim was off target and the sod landed in the Irish Sea and remains there to this day in the form of the Isle of Man - all very interesting stuff but the boating was proving to be a little uncomfortable to say the least.

Alan fought his way through the maelstrom into somewhat calmer waters just off the shores of Shanes Castle, which apparently was the home of the O'Neill Clan. The boat was put to anchor and I assembled my Fladen Maxximus 13 foot Match rod with float tackle and a size 18 hook baited with a single maggot. After a couple of minutes it was glaringly obvious that using a float was completely the wrong choice in the rough conditions. The boat was swaying to and fro in the wild water and the waves were dragging the float out of eye contact in a matter of seconds. A quick change to a paternoster leger rig didn't fare much better although I did continue to keep a trickle of feed flowing for what it was worth. I was working very hard to present the bait in the best way possible while the boat bobbed and weaved in the turbulence but it was already becoming a hopeless exercise. Alan was getting frustrated in the knowledge that under normal conditions we could have got out to his favourite marks and caught plenty of Pollan. I believe that he was more disappointed than us but there was very little he could do about it in the circumstances. We persevered for another couple of hours or so and then Alan suggested that we head back into the River Maine where we could take a breather and grab a spot of lunch.

It was a good idea to get some respite from the rolling action of the boat and the hour's break gave us time to sort ourselves out and discuss our next course of action. Alan sincerely wanted us to succeed and offered to try taking the boat out further into deeper water if we were game for a bit more discomfort. We wouldn't be able to reach his favourite marks but the depth of water would increase from the original 12 feet to about 30 feet, which might just give us the edge. Compared to the Cumbrian Lakes, the average depth of Lough Neagh was relatively shallow which I must say was a bit of a surprise to me. It certainly makes the fishing easier though because it's nigh on impossible to determine where to present the bait in water over 100 feet deep. For example it would be futile to place the bait on the bottom if the fish were feeding at a depth of 80 feet or less. Anyway getting back to the job in hand - of course we were only too happy to follow the skipper out into the tumult once again even if there was only a small chance of catching a Pollan...

When we got out past the shelter of the castle, Alan was really having to battle hard to keep the heavily pitching boat on an even keel. My head had started to spin as I looked downwards to change the lead weight for a blockend feeder and it took several minutes of focusing on the horizon to rid myself of the queasy feeling. I am rarely seasick but to have succumb on freshwater would have really let the side down. However, Rawson kept our spirits up with a string of spontaneous impersonations of Quint, Hooper and Chief from the legendary film "Jaws". One minute he was bellowing out, "We're gonna need a bigger boat" in Chief's perfect accent and a few minutes later, "Here's t'swimmin with bow-legged women" in a flawless mimic of Quint's drawl. The entertainment continued until we reached the new fishing grounds when Alan put down the anchor again. My feeder was filled with maggots before it was dropped to the floor of the Lough a few yards off the stern. Once again the severe pitch of the boat was affecting a sound presentation of the bait as the feeder continually bumped across the bottom. It was impossible to maintain a tight line so, even if bites had occurred, detection would have been impossible. Not only was the fishing difficult but as time went on the conditions seemed to deteriorate further as the wind strengthened. After a couple of hours of further exposure to the elements Alan, who had done everything possible to help us succeed, decided enough was enough. The situation was becoming hazardous and it was time to draw anchor and negotiate the return journey. It was a bitter pill to swallow but we all knew the game was over.

In summary, I had done my level best to catch a Pollan but had failed at the last hurdle. It had brought home the fact that some ventures are not always crowned with success - failure and disappointment being far more frequent. Despite the setback I was not completely deflated because I drew some satisfaction from the knowledge that "there's always tomorrow". With commitment and an open mind I'm convinced that one day a Whitefish will fall to my rod. Alan gave us the option to try again at any time during the remainder of our stay but unfortunately the strong winds continued unabated and we were unable to take him up on his offer. Nevertheless I still believe that Lough Neagh will give me the best chance to fulfil my Whitefish ambition and I shall be returning for another attempt, hopefully with Alan, in the not too distant future.

Before signing off I would like to write a few words about a couple of issues that are connected to this tale. Firstly, a brief review of the last two days of our visit which were spent sea fishing at a delightful little place named Waterfoot. We discovered this popular mark during a recce drive along the North Channel coast. It was a super venue for fishing with deep water within casting range, plenty of different fish species to go for and ample free parking on the quay itself. Using King ragworms for bait, Rawson and I accounted for numbers of Plaice, Flounder, Lesser Spotted Dogfish, Coalfish, Ballan and Corkwing Wrasse. We did not really have enough time or tackle to exploit this opportunity to the full but to a certain extent it did make up for our disappointment with the Pollan failure.

The second point: I was very heartened by the news that the authorities are now appearing to take an active interest in some of our endangered species of fish. At last, the very rare Vendace, which have been present in our waters since the Ice Age, are receiving some remedial attention in order to save them from possible extinction. I believe that they have been at risk from pollution in their remaining two Lake District domains and this has prompted the commendable action by the fishery experts. At the time of writing it is intended that 200 Vendace will be netted from Derwent Water, which currently holds about 15,000 of these fish, before they are transferred to Sprinkling Tarn. An R.A.F. helicopter equipped with special oxygenated tanks will be used to transport the fish to their new home, about seven miles away in the Borrowdale Valley. Sprinkling Tarn is thought to have the best environmental conditions for Vendace to exist and should facilitate the long-term protection of this rare species.   In addition to this consignment I understand that the authorities have collected 134,000 eggs from Derwent Water which will also be transferred in special flasks to Sprinkling Tarn.   This critical work to safeguard this historic breed of fish should be applauded by all and I sincerely wish them every success with the project.

Chapter III

Severn Surprise (18.06.2005)

I have always been a bit of a Barbel fanatic, ever since catching my first one in October 1963. My teeth were cut in my schoolboy days fishing on the old River Lea in Hertfordshire. During those early years our first job was to call into the Grocer's shop at the Old Pond, Cheshunt to beg for some stale cheese. I'm not sure if they felt sorry for us but they always seemed to come up with a sizeable square and never turned us away empty handed. After collecting the bait, the next ordeal was trying to avoid the very efficient Bailiff at the renowned fishery. We were under the age limit set by the controlling club so it was a case of keeping the lowest of profiles at all times. Only once did the Bailiff accept our two shillings for a day permit as the weather on the day was atrocious and we were literally soaked to the skin. No other anglers had been fool enough to brave the conditions and I suppose he felt that we had earned the privilege for our persistence and determination. Every day without exception during the school summer holidays was spent on the River Lea catching Chub and Barbel in the 8ozs to 1½lb range using our roving tactics. The name of the game was float trotting and it was only on rare occasions that a lead was employed. We would cast our floats into every glide and gap between the streamer weeds as we made our way along the winding contours of the river. Another good ploy was to run the float past the beds of ranunculas that grew prolifically throughout the river, although it was Chub that normally obliged there. It was great fun watching the porcupine quill which had been set slightly over depth, shoot upstream as the Barbel made off with the knob of cheese. The fishing on the Lea in those days was fabulous.

Well, that was my initiation - the Barbel progression took me to the middle reaches of the River Severn at Bewdley in Worcestershire during the mid seventies. This was the time when large bags of Barbel were the norm, falling to anglers using the "plastic pig" and feeding heavily with maggots, casters and hemp. Nowadays and during latter years my concentration has been set on the lower sections of this river between the tidal waters below Tewkesbury Weir up to Worcester City itself. Generally speaking these waters are not pressured as such and certainly have the potential to produce a very big Barbel at any time. In my opinion the very lightly fished area around Bushley would be the best place to try for one of the whackers with a night-time stint during Autumn giving the best chance. Working upstream there are other places that have provided consistent sport – Upton, Severn Stoke, Pixham and Digliss to name a few. I love the challenge of fishing in these places and spend a great deal of my time trying to winkle out the Barbel that thrive there. The one problem I do have is that I tend to keep returning to my favourite pegs instead of moving on to discover new ones, of which there are many. It was going back to one of my old haunts that gave rise to this particular tale...

As I've got older I have found it increasingly more tiring carrying all my equipment and bait to far away places on the riverbank. The physical effort of trudging through boggy fields, climbing over styles, opening and closing gates while fully loaded is very demanding. On this particular occasion I had just arrived at my chosen swim, peeled off the lumber and collapsed into my chair to recover from the hike. It was very early morning and as quiet as the proverbial grave in my secluded little dugout. I was just regaining my composure and absorbing the ambience of the scene when the peace was broken by a deafening crack as loud as a rifle shot. I nearly jumped out of my skin - in a blink of an eye, a large branch of the Willow Tree to my left had developed a 10 foot split through it's centre. It was lucky that I didn't have my rods in position as the flailing ends of the branch would have smashed them to pieces. Just my luck, a tree that had probably stood undisturbed for 20 years or more suddenly decided to shed one tonne of branch just as I had sat down beneath it!

It wasn't until later that I actually discovered that what I thought was a strange occurrence was not so strange after all. Apparently the Withy or Cracked Willow as the name suggests are in fact very prone to this "splitting" phenomenon. The timber of these large, fast-growing trees has a tendency to become hollow and brittle with age, giving rise to cracks and twists amongst the branches. Also known as the Brittle Willow, they thrive and are a common sight along the banks of our rivers.

Anyway it was June 18th and my first opportunity to fish in the new season at the Barbel Society-controlled water at Callow End. I had stowed away my headlamp and a flask so I was prepared to fish into the dark hours if the mood so took me. Most of my Barbel fishing on the Severn is done in the late Summer and Autumn months when the better fish seem to be more active. The normal routine during this period is to introduce a significant quantity of feed to stimulate them but on this occasion I had decided to rely entirely on pre-prepared PVA bags. This meant that I would be limiting the amount of free offerings available and should therefore avoid any chance of over-feeding, which in my view is a cardinal sin. The reason for this approach was because I didn't believe the Barbel would be present in numbers during this early part of the season on this section of the river. My rationale for this was that the Barbel would more likely be shoaling in the oxygenated waters of the River Teme that flows into the Severn a few miles upstream. On this particular day the Severn was running extremely low, which in a way supported my judgement. I strung up a couple of rods with the intention of only using one at a time. The first choice incorporated a running leger rig, which was finished off with a size 6 Fox Series 3 hook tied to 30 inches of ESP 10lb breaking strain braid. Main line was 12lb Maxima which is necessary in view of the snags. The bait was a hair-rigged 21mm Halibut pellet. In general I prefer running rigs with longish hook links because I tend to get more knocks and pulls before that great moment arrives when the tip wangs around in typical Barbel fashion. With conventional semi-fixed bolt rigs using heavier leads and shorter hook links, the perception of Barbel foreplay with the bait is not so evident on the quiver tip, which therefore diminishes the fun and excitement factors. Furthermore I always use the lightest lead I can get away with and this time opted for a one ounce flat lead to hold bottom in the deep water. During drought conditions when the river is hardly running at all, I have actually dispensed with the lead altogether, although a free-line does have a tendency to end up in the snags sometimes.

Anyway, when I was ready to start fishing I hooked up one of the PVA bags that had been filled with a 50/50 mix of 4mm Halibut pellets and chopped up sections of Winalot reward sticks. I've caught a few doubles on this readily available super bait but please don't tell anyone (beef flavour is the best!!) The rig was then cast into Barbel alley which lies about five yards downstream and about a quarter of the way across the river. At this location there are snags everywhere so it's important to allow the lead to settle and not to move it when tightening up the line. The Free Spirit Barbel Tamer rod was placed in the rest and I sat back to await developments - this was the exciting bit. After a few minutes the knocks on the quiver tip began and I wondered whether the Bream had moved on to the bait. The rod tip action kept me on my toes and my heart was pounding big time with expectation. Ten minutes later the tip pulled around fast and unceasingly, leaving me no time to savour the magic of the moment that all Barbel anglers crave for. I quickly grabbed the rod and lent into a powerful force.

Despite immediately applying maximum sidestrain, I failed to make any headway and the reel began to concede line as the rod hooped over in defiance. I knew the fish would surge for the heart of the snag, which was probably a branch of a tree and I tried desperately to hold it on the outer fringes to prevent a disaster. Maintaining a consistent pressure, I did manage to regain some of the line but I could feel a slight grating sensation as the Barbel tried to find sanctuary among the underwater obstructions. After a few moments of apprehension I was able to bring the fish under control and the battle continued deep down in open water more or less beneath the rod tip. It was obviously a big fish and certainly a real surprise. I had hoped to connect with a Barbel or two but had not been expecting such a lump so early in the season.

The rod was doing it's job and I was experiencing that superb "solid" feeling of a nice fish that was unhurriedly just hugging the bottom. More pressure was exerted and the fish made a few swirls before surfacing - she was mine, well almost! The fish was too long to fit into the net at first and it took a bit of jiggling before I was able to manoeuvre it through the frame. Once it was safely in the confines of the mesh, I hoisted it clear of the water and carried it to the top of the bank and laid it on the unhooking mat. The whole episode had happened so quickly and I was in a bit of a whirl. Curiously I was finding it difficult to put a quick estimate on its weight, probably due to its long, slender body. The stomach of the fish was on the flat side but I still hoped that it was going to eclipse my previous best - there was no point in guessing, the scales would let me know soon enough. Lifting my prize in the weigh-sling I watched the Avon's needle rotate around to the orange segment before settling at a weight of 12lb 9ozs. Fantastic, a new Barbel personal best taken on the first cast of the new season. Looking at the frame of the fish, I am pretty sure that it would have made 15lbs plus later in the year, given time to attain prime condition. Frustratingly there were no other anglers around so a proper photograph was out of the question and I had to settle for my usual "fish in the net" snap. I must have a drawer full of these rather meaningless pictures of fish without any real perspective of their size. One day I must invest in some professional camera kit for my trophy shots to overcome this irritating problem.

After a short period of recovery, the Barbel swam off and disappeared into the brown tinged depths. The Halibut pellet on the hair was replaced with a fresh one and I re-cast to a similar position, having already hooked up another PVA bag of goodies. An hour had passed without incident when out of the blue the tip pulled around again and I found myself connected to another Barbel - the power of the fish left me in no doubt of this fact. As before it was touch and go with snags until it was banked safely. The second fish weighed in at 9lb 5ozs - blimey I was becoming blasé!! Normality returned and all was quiet for a considerable period of time so I changed the bait for a two inch length of Winalot reward stick and soon caught a third Barbel weighing about 5lbs, which was quickly followed by another of 9lb 11ozs. "Stone the Crows" - in terms of my own fishing standards the session was turning into something bordering on the spectacular!. For the record the weather was very hot, humid and overcast - the temperature was a sultry 26°C and there was a high atmospheric pressure reading of 1032mb. Anyway, bites on the meaty sticks dried up so I reverted back once again to the 21mm Halibut pellet and this time caught a Bream weighing 8lb 2ozs - not bad for a river slab! I don't mind catching Bream of this size while I'm Barbel fishing but smaller fish in the 3-4lb bracket can sometimes become a nuisance on this water. This irritating distraction seems to be more prevalent when the target area has been primed with Halibut pellets, the Bream just cannot resist them. As evening approached I landed a 3lb Barbel that was a real speed merchant. It's uncanny how a relatively small fish can sometimes dig up so much power as to test the strongest of tackle. Likewise, the fact that it had managed to suck in a bait better chance, although I knew it would mean catching a lot of small Ballans in the process. I would just have to be patient. Sure enough, on the next cast the ragworm was taken immediately on the drop and up came a Ballan weighing less than four ounces. Sport continued in brisk fashion and I started to pull up one fish after another – this was definitely 'Wrasse a go-go'! At last, after landing nine consecutive Ballans, the tenth fish was a Corkwing, which had the telltale dark smudge on the caudle stalk. It may only have been small but I was overjoyed. One thing that surprised me was the enormous variation in the colouring of the Wrasse I was catching. I was familiar with the fact that Wrasse change their colour to blend in with their surroundings but I was casting to the same area throughout the session. I could only assume that the fish had moved in from different environments in the general locality. Anyway, by the time the tide had reached its zenith I had caught 26 Wrasse, of which three were Corkwings, and I felt it was time to call it a day. My ragworm supply had nearly been exhausted so I shouted across to my wife to say that I'd be ready to leave very shortly. The tattered bait that had been mauled by the latest fish was changed for a fresh one and I made my last cast. Bites had understandingly become more finicky by now but after a couple of minutes there was a couple of taps on the quiver and I struck into my 27th fish. I brought it to hand and couldn't believe my eyes – it was a rare Rock Cook Wrasse. This capture was really significant; I could fish for the rest of my life and not catch another one of these. The scale formation on the flanks was a beautiful burnished red-brown colour, and it had flecks of iridescent blue on the cheeks and tiny veins of the same blue colour between the eye and the angle of the mouth. Catching Corkwing had been a memorable result for me but the capture of the Rock Cook had made it a truly momentous occasion. I took some photographs and left in a haze of euphoria. A celebratory dinner for the four of us at the Five Pilchards Inn completed a perfect day.

Footnote

On arriving home it's always a pleasure for me to update my comprehensive fishing records. In the case of the Rock Cook Wrasse, I made the relevant entry, indicating the weight to be an estimated 3ozs. I was later astounded when I consulted the British Rod Caught Records Listing and found that, according to the latest schedule, the record for this fish species stands at 3ozs 13drams. As my fishing pals will confirm, I have a tendency for underestimating the weights of small fish and I shall always wonder if my catch would have beaten the current mark.

Not many of these around — a Rock Cook Wrasse

Chapter V

Mission South (12.11.2005)

Frustration was beginning to creep into my life because I had been unable to fish for Barbel at my usual haunt on the River Severn for two consecutive weeks. The setback had been harder to swallow because November was one of my favourite Barbeling months and certainly an ideal time to search for a big fish. Normally when the river is in heavy flood the fishing is good but lately it had been running so high that eight ounces was not enough to hold bottom. Within minutes of casting, the lead was being jostled out of position by a never-ending stream of flotsam that quickly accumulated on the line as an enormous volume of water surged through. During usual spate conditions six ounces of lead is sufficient to hold for 20 minutes or more before a re-cast is necessary. The situation that faced me meant that a re-cast was required every five minutes, which is not a viable fishing proposition. My friend Dave Minchew was experiencing a similar dilemma, so we decided to get our heads together and come up with an alternative arrangement - it was time to get the file out.

Thumbing through the pages we came upon an article which immediately took our eye. It was taken from an "Advanced Pole Fishing" magazine entitled "Ideology". The feature described methods used for catching Ide at a fishery near Yeovil and we wondered whether this could be the answer to our little predicament. There was a contact number for the Bailiff on the water so I telephoned him for some details and the current position as regards the Ide. He told me that the Ide were still feeding and the river was now in good order following flooding the previous week. He also advised me on the better swims but it was difficult to picture the details in my mind when I hadn't seen the place as such. Whilst I was not altogether clear on this very important part of the jigsaw, it was left that he would show me on the day. Great stuff - we were going fishing at the Old Mill Fishery on the approaching weekend and Ide would be our target. The November weather was unpredictable and we would have to pray that there would be no frost the night before our campaign.

On the day of our departure the weather forecast was for very light westerly winds with sunny periods and a temperature ranging from 5° C to 10° C - not bad at all for November. This news could not have been better and more encouragingly there hadn't been any overnight frost. We had allowed ourselves two and a half hours to make the 120-mile journey southwards and we were hoping to arrive in time for the opening of the fishery, just after first light. I had taken two rods, which I'd set up in advance and placed in the quiver bag so they would be ready for use on arrival. Saving 20 minutes or so at this time of the year when the days are relatively short is a sensible ploy which can sometimes mean the difference between success and failure. My main rod, a Drennan Team England 12 foot with action tip, was set up with a small peacock insert waggler carrying 3 x No.1 shot and finished off with a size 16 hook tied to a 2lb breaking strain hook link. The other was a light quiver rod that had been fitted with a small open-ended feeder connected in a paternoster style. My intention was to use maggots in the feeder, plugging the ends with groundbait.

Daylight had broken about half an hour before we arrived at the Old Mill, which was located in the village of Stoford. Our first job was to take a stroll around the fishery to get an idea of the layout of the place and check out the pegs. The Bailiff hadn't arrived and there was only one other angler, who was fishing in a pool lying to the right of the river that I was intending to fish. I made my way along the bank of the small river for a while, looking at likely spots to try and was pleased to see that it had plenty of features and, more importantly, a hint of colour. In a small river such as this one, stealth was a necessity and, rather than adopt a roving approach, my preference was to bring the fish to me using sensible feeding tactics. I felt that the fish would have been easily spooked if they were chased from swim to swim and that could have proved disastrous.

By now I was raring to start fishing and we quickly returned to the car to collect the gear. Dave decided to try his luck in the pool while I headed back to the river, which apparently empties into the River Yeo about a mile downstream. Making my way upstream I found a likely looking spot next to a fallen branch of a tree that had actually straddled the river. I could use the very slow movement of the flow to cover the area in front of the branch and at the same time be positioned well out of the way to avoid any disturbance. A liberal helping of loosefed maggots was introduced before I allowed the float to carry gradually into the baited area about two thirds of the way across the river. The float had got to within two feet of the ivy-covered branch before sliding away gracefully and I struck and landed a small Rudd. After releasing the fish I continued to loosefeed the target area - little and often was the name of the game. The next run though produced a Gudgeon, which was quickly followed by several others. In fact during the next hour I was catching one every cast and I must have accounted for 30 or 40 of them. The Gudgeon blitz was somewhat disconcerting and I was glad when the Bailiff turned up so that I could seek his advice. He thought my method and the light float tackle were perfect for the job but advised that the Ide were more likely to put in an appearance at the top end of the fishery. A move was welcomed and my escort helped me to transport the gear upstream towards the better swims. It was good to hear that the Ide were thriving in this little river and that they attract quite a following from anglers like ourselves who travel from far afield. The Bailiff also emphasised the importance of keeping the feed flowing in order to halt any fish passing through. He was confident that I would succeed if I stuck to the task but cautioned that I may have to be patient as it can take several hours. On reaching the far end of the fishery, we discovered that another angler had arrived and was occupying the hot peg, so I settled into the one next door. The Bailiff wished me good fortune and left me to my own devices.

I got myself organised and this time opted for a cocktail of brandling worm and maggot bait, which I hoped to some extent might deter the hordes of Gudgeon. After sprinkling a few maggots along the fishing path I swung the float into position, slightly upstream, before placing the rod in the rest. The float had been set just over depth so that the bait would just trip across the bottom very slowly with the gentle movement of the river. I watched intently as the orange, needle-like tip of the float travelled its course but no bites occurred so I repeated the exercise. Although concentrating hard, I was unable to discern any sign of fish movement whatsoever, but at least I wasn't being plagued with interfering Gudgeon that could have impeded my chances of catching an Ide. There followed almost two hours with no activity, but I kept the feed trickling in regularly. My focus was undiminished in any way or form and in the end I was rewarded for my patience with a bite that came out of the blue to the cocktail bait. It turned out to be a second Rudd and I was keeping my fingers crossed that perhaps a shoal of fish had finally entered into my patch. Five minutes later the float buried again and I struck into something more substantial. The rod was jolting and I could see the silver flanks of a nice fish jagging away in the brownish coloured water. After a few seconds the fish came to the surface and to my relief I recognised that it was indeed an Ide. The adrenalin was now pumping big time and I prayed that the barbless hook would hold as I brought it over the out-stretched net. Bingo! It was in the bag and I found it difficult to contain my glee. Before transferring the fish to the weigh sling, I gazed at its beauty for a moment as it lay motionless in the folds of the net. The blood-red fins were stunning and I called Dave over to help with the photography. The Avon scales which had been zeroed in advance showed the weight of my prize to be 1lb 3ozs and I was over the moon. Dave knew how much that fish meant to me and although he didn't say as much, that's not his style, I perceived a sense of satisfaction that I had caught the new species. Having returned the fish safely, I sat back for a few minutes to reflect and savour the moment. From my point of view taking time out of our Barbeling programme to try for the Ide had paid real dividends. The elimination of this tough target from my hit list was a major coup and completed a memorable day - as far as I was concerned it was mission accomplished!

For the record, during the remaining time I did manage to catch two smaller Ide and I lost another at the net. Recognising the potential of the Old Mill Fishery has given me the incentive to return one day to try for a 2lb fish.

Opportunity knocked for a first Ide

Chapter VI

Size Doesn't Always Matter (29.10.2005)

I had just read a really interesting article in the Anglers Mail that I immediately cut out to file, knowing that it would only be a matter of hours before I would have to take a second look. The article featured a father and son, Gary and Sam Edmonds, who had organised a very exhausting campaign to catch as many species of fish as possible within the time limit of one month. The idea was to raise cash for Children with Leukaemia and they had obviously done their homework well because they had quickly identified the venues where each target fish could be found. Drawing up their action plan was no mean feat but the challenge of the actual fishing, which required such a diversity of methods, equipment and bait, was even more demanding. Couple this with the long distance driving necessary and you can imagine the difficulty of the project. Picture setting out from home in Hertfordshire one day, travelling to North Wales and fishing hard for as long as possible before returning home and getting organised for an early morning start the following day. Arranging alternative bait and tackle, getting enough sleep, sorting food, drink and clothing etc. must have been an absolute nightmare after a couple of weeks. Anyway, they completed the task with flying colours, catching an amazing 40-plus different species, including some that were on my target list!!

Having had time to absorb all the details of their successful campaign, I decided to send them a couple of signed copies of "It started with a Perch" for their brave efforts. My thinking was that they might be able to raise some cash from the sale of these books to boost the coffers of their good cause. I was also hoping of course that they would have time to read them first as they would then discover that much of my own fishing is based on the species concept. Within a couple of days Gary and Sam got in touch to thank me for the books and we spoke at length about their experiences during their marathon project. I was particularly interested in their assault on Char and Bitterling, which are somewhat difficult to come by in British waters. I could feel my heart racing when Gary said he could show me a place on the Burwell Lode in Cambridgeshire where they had caught seven Bitterling in a relatively short period of time. This was music to my ears, even though it would mean a round journey of 300 miles from my home - quite a long way to go for a fish weighing less than an ounce.

At this juncture it would seem appropriate to break off and provide a few background details of this little fish:

The Bitterling is a small deep-bodied fish that is found in slow-flowing lowland rivers, canals and some lakes. Its habitat is dependent upon there being Swan Mussels present as it relies on these for reproduction purposes. The eggs from the female fish are actually laid inside the living mussel via a long tube that is developed during the breeding period. The male fertilises the eggs by releasing sperm near the mussel, which gets sucked inside as it breathes. The Bitterling is an ornamental pond and aquarium fish and is not native to British waters. However it did become established in St Helens, Lancashire in the 1920's and more recently in the Shropshire Union Canal, Cambridgeshire Lodes as well as some waters in Lancashire and Cheshire. On the continent it is fairly widespread from the eastern edge of France to the basins of the Black and Caspian Seas. The British rod caught record is held by Dennis Flack with a fish weighing 12 drams taken from Barway Lake in Cambridgeshire in 1998 ···.

I knew Gary's kind gesture to show me the actual

whereabouts of the fish was half the battle won — location is the key. However, I was a little concerned about the timing of a trip as it was the end of October and there had been a fair amount of flooding across the country. I was reluctant to travel such a long distance for fear of failing due to the adverse conditions. My mind was torn between a yearning to try my luck without delay and postponing the trip until the following summer when the circumstances would be more ideal. In view of the situation, Gary agreed to telephone his contact who lived in the area in order to get an up-to-date report on the state of affairs. Local contacts are worth their weight in gold and I was relieved, if not a little surprised, when he came back with some favourable feedback. Apparently there was a tinge of colour in the water and it was slightly up on normal levels but the general prospects remained good and there was still a chance of catching Bitterling. One slight setback, however, was that the authorities had recently completed their annual task of cutting the bank-side vegetation along the entire stretch of the fishery. It appears that much of the green waste ends up in the margins of the drain, which can have an adverse affect on the fishing. This was only a minor issue to me, and having weighed up all the information to hand, I was already champing at the bit to give it a try – a decision to go the following weekend was made ….

On the day I picked up my brother-in-law, Phil Woolard, in Broxbourne, before travelling on to meet Gary and Sam. Following the formalities we set off for the Cambridgeshire Fens, which was about an hour's drive away. When we got within a few miles of the venue, the landscape changed notably and became very flat, reminding me of the fenland area surrounding the Norfolk Broads. We had certainly been very lucky with the weather as there was a light south westerly breeze and a balmy autumn temperature of 17°c – more importantly there had been no frost. It wasn't long before we approached the sluice gate at the start of the fishery where we paused for a while to get a general feel for the place. The canal-like drain was about 10 yards wide and stretched out uniformly into the open countryside. On the far bank there were several boats and barges moored and I could only see four other anglers dotted about – this was great news. Gary pointed out the exact spot where Sam had caught the Bitterling previously and I jumped out of the car to have a closer look. Peering into the margins I could see a shoal of small fish that resembled junior Roach and wondered if I had found the elusive target. Losing no more time we parked the car and made our way back to the spot about 40 yards downstream of the sluice gate to assemble our tackle for the short session.

On our arrival one of the anglers fishing between the barges on the far bank came across to issue the £5 day tickets. He informed us that the Perch were currently going mad and that he had caught four fish in excess of 3lbs and a countless number of 2's on small live baits. I love catching big Perch and I listened intently to what he was saying but realised that any serious assault on the Perch would have to wait for another day. This was very impressive stuff and in light of the news, Phil decided to use worms for bait on float tackle and Gary set up a lure rod. Sam and I assembled our whips with ultra light tackle for the Bitterling. My end tackle consisted of a tiny float cocked with a single micro-shot and a size 24 hook attached to a 14 ounce hook link! Blimey, this was a million miles away from my usual method, as I would normally use a size 6 Raptor for the Barbel. With everything ready I selected a tiny pink maggot for bait and had some difficulty fumbling about trying to mount the thing on the microscopic hook. I could barely see it, let alone bait it. The moment of truth had arrived and I lowered the pink morsel gently into the margins, just over what was remaining of the bank side rushes. The little pink beacon of light began to fade as it sank away slowly through the dark water. My eyes were straining to see the bait drop down to the critical zone when all of a sudden it disappeared from view altogether and I struck instinctively. Up came a small fish that I quickly swung into my hand and bingo, I was looking down at a Bitterling. You could have knocked me down with a feather. After all the preparations, I had cracked the target within 10 seconds of starting to fish. Was I a happy bunny or what? It may have only weighed a few drams but it meant the world to me!

During the short session, Phil and Gary enjoyed plenty of sport catching Perch and Pikelets while Sam and I pulled in a steady flow of small Bream, Perch, Roach, Rudd and of course Bitterling. This super fishery controlled by the Cambridge Fish Preservation and Angling Society has much to offer and has certainly got a lot of big fish potential. I for one will definitely be investing in a season permit next year with a view to having a bash at those big Stripeys!

A belting Bitterling!!!

Chapter VII

Carpin' On (28.10.2004)

We try to get away at least once a year these days and this time my old buddy Richard Fobbester and I had booked a week's guided fishing at Mequinenza in Spain. There are a fair number of guiding services now operating in the area but we chose to stick with Colin Bunn of Catmaster Tours, who is totally dependable and has certainly come up trumps for us on previous visits. The beauty of this kind of arrangement is that the vast majority of the specialist fishing paraphernalia required is supplied for you, which makes air travel a feasible option. Colin caters for anglers who are interested in catching either Wels Catfish or Carp and on this trip we had chosen to fish for Carp. The reason for this decision was because it was the end of October and the best of the Cat fishing was fast coming to an end. Also, we were both looking for a 30lb river Carp, which is always a possibility at Mequinenza. The timing of the trip was deliberate, as we didn't want to experience a repeat of the terrible fly problem of the summer months again. Unfortunately we got it wrong again and were in fact eaten alive by the little devils.

All the arrangements went like clockwork until we were approaching the point of no return at the airport. We were both wearing coats that had every pocket laden with fishing bits including an assortment of four and five ounce lead weights. As expected, we were ushered over by the security personnel - this situation is now accepted as an occupational hazard and part of the game when travelling overseas. Quite reassuringly they went through all our belongings with a fine toothcomb, to find that, unbeknown to us at the time, we had committed a cardinal sin. The line on our big pit reels, stored in our hand luggage to protect them from damage, was considered a lethal weapon. We explained that we would be unable to go on a fishing holiday without them and after a bit of conciliation, I was allowed to go back to a special check-in desk to resubmit the offending items, including a whole load of lead! It may have been a lot of hassle but it was a big relief to know that this critical part of our equipment was coming with us, albeit in the hold of the aircraft. Job done.

At Barcelona Airport we made our way to the big bronze statue of the Bull, which was Colin's normal meeting place. Here we met up with the other four anglers who had booked with Colin for the same week. It was incredible to think that within a matter of a few hours we would all be on the bank somewhere, beginning our campaigns to catch a monster. Whatever happened from this point on Richard and I knew that even if the fishing wasn't up to scratch we would at least have a good laugh and enjoy the welcome break from work. Right on cue Colin arrived to chauffeur us in the people carrier to our accommodation in Mequinenza, about a two hour drive away. During the general fishing banter it emerged that the fishing was a little patchy at present. There were a few big Carp around but the quantity of smaller fish around the 20lb mark was on the low side. Furthermore, most of the captures were occurring in the early morning or later in the evening when the fish seemed to be more active. Conversely, the Catfish prospects remained good which was pleasing news for Jeff Edisbury, the one member of our party who had taken the "Silurus" option.

Obtaining the necessary fishing licences in Spain can be a bit of a headache so it was heartening to know that Colin had already arranged them in advance - all part of the service. From my point of view the only downside was the fact that the authorities did not allow night fishing for Carp.

I believe there is a slight concession for the Catfish Anglers who are able to fish later into the evening but at the time of writing there is no fishing allowed throughout the night. The consensus of opinion was that the six of us would begin our programme on the Rio (River) Segre where a few fish had been showing here and there. To acquaint ourselves with the venue, Colin thought it would be a good idea to take us along the chosen stretch to see the available pegs before continuing on to the apartment in the heart of Mequinenza. The journey time seemed to fly by and before we knew it Colin was pausing at all the hot spots on the Segre where each of us selected our pegs for the next morning. There were a fair number of Spanish anglers present, who seemed to be using an armoury of rods and I was a little concerned about finding enough room to fish. Colin explained that it was still the weekend, when most of the local boys come out in force to try their luck, and he didn't envisage any problems the following day. All sorted, our harmonious team of enthusiasts moved back to base to organise the tackle, bait and sleeping quarters. Each pair of anglers was allocated a 50-inch landing net, unhooking mat, Carp sack, weigh sling, Reuben Heaton scales for weights up to 120lbs, bed chair, shelter, throwing stick, a couple of rod pods and a pair of 3¼lb test curve Carp rods - all top quality gear, can't be bad! The only other task was the drilling of a bucketful of Halibut pellets so that they would be ready for rigging first thing the following morning. Everything was ready by late evening so we headed into town to grab some tucker and a few beers in Colin's bar - life couldn't have been better...

Day One – Rio Segre

Colin arrived at the apartment to ferry us to the swims about an hour before daybreak, around 6am, so we could maximise the fishing time. Each pair had been given a designated time for collection, which was done in shifts at 15-minute intervals. The idea was to make sure the rods were ready for casting at the first sign of light, which was the most likely time to get a bite. The end tackle consisted of a semi-fixed rig using heavy-duty Korda safety clips in conjunction with a four-ounce lead. The hook link was a six-inch length of 25lb Quicksilver braid, which was finished off with a size 2 hook. Main line was 15lb Maxima and the bait was a pair of 22mm Halibut pellets hair-rigged and supported with a small PVA bag containing samples of the same bait. Casting long distance wasn't an issue on the Segre so there was no problem using PVA, which can cut the casting range considerably. The target fishing ground lay in the region of 60 to 70 yards away on a gradually rising shelf - a doddle for the Shimano big pit reels. We were casting across the deeper channel that ran close to the nearside of the river where apparently many of the Catfish are caught. Richard and I were fishing within a few yards of each other and the problems began as soon as we had cast and settled the rods. We assumed that the River Authorities had been carrying out a weed cutting exercise somewhere upstream because huge rafts of weed were floating down with the current and snagging the line. There was so much of it that it couldn't be avoided and a re-cast was necessary every 10 minutes or so. We tried propping up the rods beach-caster style, sinking the rod tip below the surface and fishing the deep water cut close in but all proved to be a waste of time. By lunchtime we had had enough and decided to telephone Colin to ask for a move to a different section of the river system. By the time we had packed away all the gear and got set up again in our new environment there was only a few hours remaining to fish before it got dark.

The new venue was situated on an old road that disappeared into the depths of the River Ebro, presumably due to dam building activity further along the river and the subsequent flooding of the land. The outlook here was just wonderful with clear skies, rolling hills and a castle perched on top of the hill behind us. At this juncture it's worth mentioning the birdlife of this region, which is an ornithologist's dream. On most days it's not unusual to see Eagles soaring and very impressive Storks riding the thermals way above the river and surrounding plains. Using binoculars these birds are a truly awesome spectacle. Storks have always held a kind of sentimental value and it is of no surprise that the nest built on the church roof in the middle of town is an important tourist attraction. We had made time during our previous visit to Mequinenza to view the nest-site but unfortunately the Storks weren't in residence, probably having already raised their young earlier. Other special memories of the feathery kind were seeing Nightingales, exquisite looking Bee-eaters and a Marsh Harrier that Colin pointed out as it quartered the reed-beds on the far bank of the river. Reverting back to the fishing ... Richard had one run just before dark which resulted in our first fish, an 18lb Common. We had seen enough potential to return to the same place the following day.

Day Two – Rio Ebro (The Disappearing Road)

We were again all set up and ready to start before first light in the prime spot where the road meets the edge of the water. The water here was very deep on the inside, perhaps 35-40 feet, but as before there was a shelf of shallower water in casting range further out. Behind us on the other side of the disappearing road a small pool of comparatively still water had been created which also looked to have a nice depth to it. The shoals of Bleak that had gathered there were continuously being harassed from below by predators. I assumed the culprits were Zander although I had seen a couple of Bass leaping clear of the water on occasions. Colin said these would have been the Large Mouthed variety, which was a species high on my hit list, but these would have to wait for another time - the strict authorities would certainly not tolerate use of a third rod. After a few hours of inactivity, the sun came out and with it came the flies - it was a scorcher and was not as we had

CAST A CLEVER LINE

expected. Furthermore, just above our position where the road rises from the water, a group of about 30 local students had joined us to fish. They were crammed in like sardines and employed a wide range of tackle and methods. It was fun watching them catch small Carp, Bleak and a whole load of Zander between the maze of criss-crossed lines throughout the confined area. Unfortunately this was the only entertainment that Richard and I had - while the students' strings were constantly being pulled, ours remained motionless for the duration. Prospects were not looking too bright.

During the drive back to the apartment it was good to hear that Jeff had scored with a 112lb Catfish taken on the Segre although the rest of the party, like us, were struggling with the Carp. Over dinner the question of where to fish the following day was discussed and the options narrowed down to two. It was either Pedro's Orchard on the Ebro or behind the Water Treatment Works on the Segre - we chose the latter.

Sitting at the end of the disappearing road

Day Three – Rio Segre (Water Treatment Plant)

Walking around the perimeter fence of the Water Works in the dark, fully loaded with fishing gear, proved to be a bit tricky. One careless step could have meant a tumble down the embankment into the Segre, so it was a relief when we arrived at the end pegs by the bridge unscathed. On our safe arrival however, we were slightly distracted by the fact that we had disturbed something resembling a large cat on the prowl. We had often heard these secretive animals in the thick margin undergrowth but apart from a brief glimpse of their eyes illuminated in a torch beam now and then, they had eluded us. One thing was for sure though - the stench around the place was appalling but I suppose that should have been expected as we were fishing alongside a sewerage farm. Colin explained that a long cast was a necessity in order to reach the deeper channel which began at the third arch of the bridge. Allowing for the lead to settle, we estimated that a cast of 100 yards would comfortably put us into the target zone - no problem. We dispensed with the PVA to facilitate casting the distance and did the baiting up using the throwing stick. Of course we also had the option of introducing bait into the zone from the top of the bridge if we felt it was necessary. After about two hours without so much as a bleep, we both reeled in to find the baits on all four rods were missing. This was a bit of a mystery which we could only put down to the failure of the bait bands that we were using to hold the pellets on the hair. It was strange though that no problems had been experienced previously when we had been casting shorter distances. For a test run the hairs were re-baited using the bands again and following their recovery five minutes later, we found the baits had come adrift a second time - a lesson had been learned, it was back to conventional boilie stops.

Nothing stirred, apart from the nauseous odour, until mid-afternoon when one of Richard's rods was away. As soon as he picked up the rod the fish went to ground and he was unable to budge it, despite trying all the normal tricks of the trade to free up the tackle. After a few minutes of slack lining without result he decided to climb up onto the bridge in order to get beyond the fish, which he hoped was still on the hook. Richard walked up to the fourth arch, tightened up the line and luckily managed to free the fish from the snag. Within a few more minutes he had coaxed it back to our bank where I netted his second Common Carp weighing 24lb 12ozs. No more bites occurred until about an hour before we were due to pack up, when one of my alarms announced my first bite at long last. I rushed over, lifted the rod, simultaneously disengaging the bait runner, and immediately felt the power of something very significant at the end of the line. The top section of the rod pulled over violently as the fish took off at speed and I suddenly found myself on the back foot struggling for control. Line was being conceded against the clutch of the reel but unfortunately it was too little too late and after a matter of seconds I experienced that sickening sensation of the line parting company. I couldn't believe the fish had actually broken 15lb line at a range of 100 yards and that I hadn't even been given enough time to switch off the anti-reverse. It had all happened so quickly and I was choked and very annoyed with myself. The clutch had been set too tightly and I had paid a dear price - there could be no excuses. At the time I had assumed the culprit was a Catfish but in hindsight I believe it was probably a big Carp – anyway, it wasn't my day.

In fact it wasn't my night either - my other obsession is eating and I'm always game for trying out the "unusual", but I wish I hadn't tried this one. I had overheard someone raving about "pigs' ears" which was a speciality served in a little bar-restaurant just across the way from Colin's Bar. I couldn't contemplate leaving Mequinenza without sampling the local delicacy so I thought I would give it a whirl. When the waiter presented me with the meal I looked in horror at the putrid mound of gristle that filled the plate before me. I glanced across at Richard to gauge his reaction and as predicted he was nearly wetting himself. More galling was the fact that he exaggerated the point of protecting his own mouth-watering dinner with outstretched arms as if I had been about to rob him of a good part of it. There was no way I could have attempted to eat my own meal so I sat back and watched Richard devour his steak and chips with gusto. Bon appetite mate!

Day Four – Rio Ebro, Pedro's Orchard

It was dark and raining when Colin dropped us off to fish on the fourth day, so the shelter was given priority over the rods on this occasion. Since arriving in Mequinenza, Richard had been looking forward to casting a line at Pedro's Orchard because he had brought a lot of fish to the scales there on his previous visit. It was a new venue for me and I was looking forward to the challenge. There was just enough room on the small gravel peninsula for two anglers, maybe three with a squeeze, and we were fortunate that the place was vacant. The rods were cast and placed in the pods and within two minutes my left hand alarm was screaming. There was a satisfying solid resistance when I lifted the rod and this time I made sure the anti-reverse was switched off, just in case of any sudden surges. It felt like a good fish and whilst I didn't want to hurry it too much for fear of losing it, I was anxious to get my first Kipper in the net. The fish had kited way off to the left, away from the other lines, so I told Richard not to bother reeling in the other rods. Despite the lack of space, avoiding the other lines had not been a problem and soon the Common was wallowing in the shallows ready to be netted. Gripping the mesh of the net, Richard lifted the fish across to the unhooking mat where we looked at it in the half-light of dawn. My immediate thought was that it might go over the magical 30lb barrier but I didn't want to tempt providence so I kept quiet. The scales were zeroed appropriately and Richard shone the torch on the dial as I held the fish aloft, awaiting the moment of truth. The fish had been a long time coming and the wait was worth every minute - it weighed a fraction under 31lbs and I was on cloud nine. During the next hour we had four more fish between us. Richard took Commons of 25lb 10ozs and 21lbs dead and I had a Common of 22lb 8ozs and a tiny Wels Catfish that was less than 2lbs. After the early morning rush the sport went quiet and, frustratingly, from about 7.45am until we departed at dusk there was no further action, but we were looking forward to returning the following morning.

Richard displays a couple of 20's from Pedro's peninsula

Day Five – Rio Ebro, Pedro's Orchard

For our second bout of fishing at this place we decided to swap our positions from the previous day, just for the sake of making things even. Richard set his stool on the point to the left and I fished towards the reed beds on the right. Once again it was still dark when we arrived but at least it wasn't raining, so we could get the rods sorted out straight away. I was very confident of action early on again and, sure enough, within five minutes we both had screaming runs and were battling fish together. My fish appeared to be the smaller of the two so I set about landing it first to clear the way for Richard's fish. It was straightforward enough and I was able to pass the net on to Richard, who also landed his fish without problem. They were both Commons and weighed 20lb 9ozs and 26lb 12ozs respectively. The hectic action continued until about 8am when things went quiet, as before. During the "hot" period three more 20-pounders were caught - Richard took two of them, 23lb 14ozs and 20lb 8ozs, and I had one, which was 20lbs on the button. It looked more like a day when we were going to get a lot more sunbathing done than active fishing but whatever was in store, it certainly beat working.

We had heard through the grapevine about a famous Fig Tree, which was reputed to bear fantastic fruit so we decided to explore our little patch to see if we could find it. Sure enough we discovered it growing near Pedro's little cottage, but before plundering the large green figs we thought it best to have a word with Pedro first. Communication wasn't easy but with Richard's pidgin Spanish together with plenty of gesticulation and sign language we finally heard the magic words "Si Senor" which we hoped had given us the green light. The figs were absolutely divine and we ate a stack of them throughout the course of the day but, oh boy, did we pay for it later. Neither of us got much sleep that night and the toilet at the apartment certainly worked overtime!!!

Anyway, uncharacteristically, at noon one of my alarms began to bleep out the good news of another take. I rushed over to pick up the rod and immediately had to start back-winding to avoid another powerful fish causing a breakage. After tearing off on its initial run the battle settled down to one of those unhurried but very solid affairs. The fish then kited a fair distance towards the left and Richard had to reel in both his rods rapidly to prevent the fish picking up his lines and dragging the heavy lead weights. I've lost a few good fish in this way before when fishing in a confined area and didn't want any repeat. Thankfully there were no problems this time and the fight continued in open water. I was dying to get a glimpse of the fish but it stayed deep until I had brought it to within about a dozen yards of the bank, when it surfaced momentarily. It was the width across its shoulders that struck me first and then the fact that it was grounding when it was still five yards from shore. The power of these river Carp was phenomenal and even now I was unable to relax the pressure in any way for a moment. Richard waded out a few yards to overcome the grounding problem and after a few more attempts to escape, the big Common was netted. As it lay on the unhooking mat I knew that it was going to be a lifetime best and so it proved to be - 35lb 14ozs. The drinks were on me!

Lifetime best river Carp — 35lb14ozs

Day Six (The Last Day) - Rio Ebro, Pedro's Orchard

Lack of sleep was catching up with us but we couldn't afford to take a lie-in and risk missing the "juicy" time when most of our fish had been caught. We were both feeling below par because of drinking too much beer the night before to celebrate my catch and of course eating too many figs! However we had made sure that we were ready for the early morning pick-up and were bankside in good time for first light. It looked like it was going to be hot again but that didn't mean we could leave the thermal underwear at home. The extremes of temperature were not easy to cope with at this time of the year because for the first few hours each morning it was literally freezing cold but later on it invariably turned out hot enough to fry an egg. Mentioning fiery weather conditions has reminded me of our very first visit to Mequinenza, when the heat was unbearable for the duration of our trip which could have ended in disaster - I shall just digress a while:

We had been camping on the banks of the Segre close to the protected wildlife area at the time of the incident. The temperature had remained in the forties and everything was tinder-box dry. Our party of anglers was having a great time but the actual fishing had been slow due to extremely low oxygen levels arising from a river running well below the norm. It was so hot that even attempting to sleep during the night in the open air was a complete waste of time. Anyway, one morning someone spotted a family of Wild Boar grazing on the far bank, probably 600 yards or more distant and we were sharing the binoculars to see the rare event. When the piglets came out of hiding, one of the lads volunteered to take a couple of our cameras out in a rubber dinghy to try and get some photographs. He had ventured out perhaps half way when all of a sudden he turned tail and paddled furiously back to the bank. There was some urgency in his voice when he informed us that he had seen a huge firestorm approaching our position from behind. We had been unable to see it, being tucked into the steep bank, but it was coming at quite a rate of knots and we had to evacuate immediately or face the possibility of being incinerated. This was a serious fire that had apparently wiped out several homesteads in its path across the hills. As we were trying to gather our thoughts the police arrived and instructed us to leave before we had time to collect our belongings. Eight of us literally dived into a Volvo estate car to make our escape into Mequinenza. I'll never forget the noise of the fire spreading towards us, consuming all in its track including trees that vanished in minutes. In fact it was quick thinking by Colin that saved the day and our kit. Returning straightaway to the scene in a boat, he managed to penetrate the area of our little campsite to salvage our belongings, together with all the specialist fishing equipment. Well done that man!

Getting back to the fishing - the early period had been hectic but short-lived once again. Richard had taken three more 20-pounders and had nearly achieved his first 30. The statistics for his morning's catch were: 23lb 8ozs, 29lb 11ozs and 27lb 4ozs. My tally of two fish included a tiddler of 7lb 12ozs and another of 21lb 5ozs. The former fish would certainly have made a good livebait for a Catfish had we got the appropriate tackle and, of course, a boat. Anyway, apart from catching a Bleak on a lobworm while messing around with a modified piece of bamboo cane and a homemade reed float, there was no further action on our autumn break.

A summary of our results suggests that the fish count had been low by Ebro standards but the quality of the fish had certainly made the trip to Spain worthwhile. We hadn't chosen the best time to go for the Carp but from our point of view the outcome had been rewarding. It was a pity that the Carp activity was mainly restricted to such short early morning periods because it meant that for 95% of the time we were twiddling our thumbs. However this was a fact of life and something we had to accept and is very typical of how fishing can be sometimes. I shall look forward to returning again one day in the future and hopefully with Colin as my guide.

+++++

This story wouldn't be complete without saying a few words about Colin Bunn who was one of the "pioneers" of Wels Catfishing on the Rio Ebro - so here goes:

Soon after discovering the fishing potential of the river, Colin relocated to Mequinenza to set up his guiding business, Catmaster Tours, in the heart of the Spanish wilderness. Despite intense competition from an ever-growing band of would-be experts, Colin has managed to remain at the forefront of guiding at this angling Mecca. His own record of captures speaks volumes, with 187 Catfish over 100lbs and two over 200lbs, with a top fish weighing in at 212lbs. This is not to forget his largest true Albino Catfish that turned the scales to a very creditable 151lbs. There is every possibility that these very impressive statistics have already been superseded as I write. Over the years I have been struck by his knowledge and devotion to his profession, but it is his commendable stance on the welfare of these fine fish that has always lodged in my mind. It is a real eye-opener to see him working his magic to soothe a large Catfish struggling for its life after it has been brought to shore. His gentle handling and apparent empathy with these huge beasts prior to their safe return is remarkable. To emphasise the point, I have known him to actually swim out and dive down several times to release Catfish when they have become snagged on the bottom of the river during the battle to land them. This very dangerous procedure in order to save the life of a tethered Catfish can take considerable time and energy. Considering the distance, depth and the powerful current of this mighty river, one can begin to gauge a better understanding of the character of this modest and courageous man.

Colin Bunn with a 201lb Ebro Catfish

Chapter VIII

Searching For Silver (27.05.2005)

If I had just one fish on my target list that has proved extremely elusive over the years, it would be the Herring. Having witnessed a few of my mates catch them randomly here and there, I thought it would only be a matter of time before one homed in on my lure. Nevertheless as time passed by without even a hint of a Silver Bar, catching a Herring gradually became a high priority objective. In an attempt to overcome this rather difficult challenge, I carried out a fair amount of research and experimentation but still failed miserably time after time as each fishing opportunity arose. Most of my unsuccessful attempts were made casting from the rocks at Porthkerris Point in Cornwall where I knew Herring had been encountered by other anglers fishing for Mackerel. However, despite following the best advice available and being fully prepared I was still unable to locate a shoal with my choice of tackle. To be honest, there didn't appear to be any common denominator and the fishing seemed to be a bit of a lottery. The general consensus of the experts was that fishing on a high tide at dusk would provide the best chance, but in practice this tactic only produced Mackerel for my efforts. Another dodge was ripping the lures at speed through the upper layers of the sea but this method failed for me as well. In fact I tried many different approaches, using umpteen types of feather and shrimp lures, but all to no avail.

Another avenue opened when I gleaned some sound information from an article written by the versatile and very knowledgeable Mike Thrussell in one of the popular angling papers. Mike, who is a master at catching different species, had apparently been successful in sorting out a few Herring using artificial flies normally associated with Trout fishing. I believe that the patterns in question were Red Tag and Bloody Butcher. Of course my immediate response was to purchase a few samples via the Internet so that I would be ready on my next trip to Porthkerris - but you've guessed it, I only caught Mackerel! I must say though, there were a few occasions when I thought that a Herring might have been hooked, only to find after recovering the line that the culprit was a small Pollack or Greater Sandeel. My pal Rawson has actually caught two Herring on different occasions at Porthkerris on Silver Shrimp lures and he doesn't let me forget the fact either! To rub it in further, I met an angler in May 2004 who had caught four of the blighters in one short session, again at Porthkerris. At the time the news gave me some heart but the feeling was shortlived because I couldn't get a sniff of one myself, despite thrashing the place for hours. Inwardly I had thrown in the towel, believing that the only way I could succeed was to hit on a random shoal while out boat fishing. However the chances of this happening were very slim indeed, as I rarely have the time and opportunity to do much boat fishing these days. The task could take forever...

However, it was during our family holiday in May 2005 that my luck took a turn for the better. Rawson and I had made an extra early start in order to arrive at Porthkerris during the high tide period, with the idea of fishing for an hour before returning with enough Mackerel to feed the rest of the family a hearty breakfast. It was before 6am when we arrived but we hadn't expected the place to be cloaked in semi-darkness. There was low cloud and a heavy sea mist wafting slowly towards us on the calm air from the direction of Falmouth. Strangely, there were no other anglers on site and we were able to secure our favourite rock position. An eerie silence had fallen across the bay and even talking between ourselves seemed louder than normal and we felt that we had to lower our voices to maintain the peace. The waters here are very deep and one day I would

All that waiting and then two come along at once!

Chapter IX

Arctic Challenge (26.07.2006)

I'll come clean right away and explain that this tale is not about a jaunt to the North Pole or Lapland but an expedition to try and connect with the elusive Arctic Char. It might sound like a straightforward exercise but this little ambition of mine will involve a lot of time and commitment and the prospect of failure could be said to be almost inevitable. Even some of our leading, high profile anglers oozing with talent and resources have struggled with this one in U.K. waters. The problem is that these fish are very scarce and, like Whitefish, tend to live in large, deep-water lakes where access is not always a matter of routine.

A story about fishing for Arctic Char would not be complete without mentioning the handful of renowned Char-men who have used their specialist skills to land a number of these fish over the years. These dedicated boatmen apply their trade using traditional methods that have been honed to perfection particularly on Lake Windermere and Coniston Water in Cumbria. Trolling the depths with their carefully selected lures, they have made this rather romantic style of fishing their own. Looking across the calm waters of the lake at dawn from the quay at Bowness, I have often watched the silhouettes of these folk at work rowing over the fishing grounds amid the early morning mist. In order to obtain some insider knowledge of this unique pursuit, I contacted Martin Cooper who is an exponent and "leading light" among the Char fishermen of Windermere. His expertise and consistent catch rates are second to none. In fact Martin is related to the late J.B.Cooper who is recognised by the Char fishing fraternity as the "Godfather" of this traditional form of angling. Martin gave me a brief overview of the equipment used nowadays beginning with the bamboo fishing poles, which range between 16 and 18 feet in length. Main line is normally braid in excess of 100lb breaking strain, which leads us on to the critical part of the system, the "plumb". This is the specially designed weight that I believe was originally developed by J.B.Cooper to hold the business end of the tackle in place at the required depth. I understand there are now two versions of the plumb, the "Cone" and the "Pinder". These have been shaped specifically so as to give them some movement as they are trolled through the deep water. It is felt that the movement of the plumb provides a better catch rate compared to using a regular shaped weight that only follows a straight line. For the record the average depth of Lake Windermere is 78½ feet which has given rise to the fact that most of the Char fishing folk set their tackle to a depth of around 80 feet. Martin mentioned shackles, swivels, rings and intermediary sections of line that are all part and parcel of the set-up but, for the sake of simplicity, I'll get straight on to the business end of the rig. The final spinner trace is normally three yards long and in Martin's case he uses a relatively heavy 15lb line for the purpose because of possible attacks by Ferox Trout. Choice of lure appears to be a personal thing and perhaps a guarded part of their proud tradition. The special lures are all hand made and come with names given by their inventors such as the "Cooper Bomb". Others include the "Jet" which apparently is complex to make, the lesser known but highly effective "Pighead" and the widely used "Tailbait". On the face of it the logical approach for me to try for a Char would seem to be to team up with someone like Martin. However this option couldn't be further from my mind - allow me to explain.

In my view any fish caught on these boats are the result of the skills and actions of the boatmen alone and no part of the catch should be attributed to any passengers. To sit in the boat and simply pull in a fish already hooked by the efforts of the boatman does not count in my book. I for one would certainly not lay claim to any fish caught in this way. As far as I am concerned the boatman is responsible for setting the lines, manoeuvring the boat for the best presentation of the bait and ultimately any fish that are boated – period. It's a real pity though because there is nothing I would like better than to venture out on these beautiful waters for an early morning bout of Char fishing. However, in view of the aforementioned remarks this option has to be cast aside and removed from the agenda.

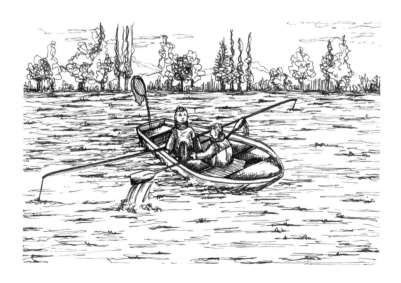

"Char-fishing" by Nicci Booth

Despite the fact that I have not been fortunate enough to connect with a Char yet, it has not been for the want of trying. I have actually travelled around the Cumbrian Lakes on a number of occasions looking for bank anglers in the hope that someone can pass on some sort of inspiration. However, on all my travels only once did I come into contact with a serious angler. He happened to be fishing for Brown Trout and Char on Lake Buttermere with tackle that wouldn't have been out of place perched on the bank of the local Carp pool. The chap had just settled in his bivvy, having launched large maggot feeders a good 80 yards or more, when I approached him to pick his brains. His set-up was certainly impressive and somewhat unexpected in this environment. A pair of Carp rods fitted with big pit reels sat on a pukka pod with Delkim alarms and swingers - this guy had really gone for the whole nine yards, as they say. The encounter was very welcome and I was able to glean some valuable information, which was a big step forwards in my campaign. However, in practice, my newly acquired knowledge didn't actually put any Char on the scales, although over time I did manage to catch a number of Brown Trout from the very deep waters. To have scored at all in this wild, open environment was encouraging and a minor victory of sorts but with no Char showing I began to get increasingly demoralised as time passed by. The obsession with this fish must have really been getting to me as I remember finding myself gawping at a few of them displayed neatly on the slab in the window of a wet-fish shop in Windermere. I must have immediately become mesmerised as I also remember my rather agitated wife dragging me away and breaking my dream of catching just one of them - blimey I must remember to get a life sometime, sad plonker!

My quandary continued until I met up with Gary and Sam Edmonds mentioned in the earlier chapter, "Size Doesn't Always Matter", who gave me a new angle to pursue. During their own species hunt they had fished for Char in

Llyn Padarn, which lies in the foothills of Mount Snowdon in North Wales. Whilst they didn't score in the limited time they had available there, Gary did in fact hook a Char on a trolled spinner, which unfortunately threw the hook at the net. This was an exciting development and I collated all the relevant contact details including the Secretary of the local club - Seiont, Gwyr Fai and Llyfni Angling. Wasting no time, I got in touch with their top man Huw Hughes right away for a general chat so I could decide upon my next course of action. I couldn't have hoped for a better contact and through him I was able to arrange caravan accommodation, the booking of a boat and battery engine for a couple of days as well as all the necessary fishing permits. It's not a bad ploy to get as much as possible organised in advance as it certainly reduces the risk of any last minute panics arising. The trip was also a good opportunity for a bout of sea fishing if time allowed so I thought I would get in touch with my buddy Rawson Bradley who is partial to dropping a line in the briny, to see if he wanted to join me on this mission. He had a kind of sarcastic smile set on his dial as he listened to my fishy proposal and I wasn't sure if he was going to buy it. I knew he was a glutton for punishment but I felt sure the rough trip to Lough Neagh the previous year would have a negative bearing on his decision. In fact the thought of taking a step away from our usual fishing comfort zones appealed to him and I was taken by surprise a little when he jumped at the opportunity. This was great news, Raws was definitely up for the challenge and our diaries were marked for a bash in July...

The weather was scorching as we drove up the A5 towards our destination - astonishingly the temperature gauge in the car was reading 37°c!!! We were heading for our base at the Snowdon Fricsan Inn that lies at the western end of Llyn Padarn to park our touring caravan. This was the perfect location to facilitate our assault on the Arctic Char. We had arranged to leave the first day free which would give us time to get our bearings before spending the following two days afloat.   We also wanted to meet up with Huw Hughes in order to get the latest information on the fishing. On arrival I telephoned him to arrange a meeting but was taken aback to hear that he had suffered a severe leg injury the day before and was virtually immobile. Despite his pain and discomfort he was kind enough to invite us to his home so we could tie up all the loose ends. The poor chap could have done without our intrusion but it wasn't long before we were all deeply engrossed in conference and enjoying the fishy banter. It quickly became evident that we had found the right man to help us with our tough challenge. Huw's knowledge was invaluable to us and I loved the enthusiastic manner in which he put it across. He marked our ordnance survey map with the best places to try some trolling on the lake and also the position of the buoys that had been installed specially for the purpose of jigging with maggots for Char. It came to light that we also had the option to fish in Llyn Cwellyn which was about 10 miles drive southwards. The Char here were smaller than their Padarn brethren but it was certainly an alternative worth considering. As luck had it, the electric boat engine, battery and fishing licenses had to be collected from the pub in the adjoining village so at least we could get a good look at the place in advance. Huw sorted us out some anti-kink leads and some Mepps Comet spinners in the larger sizes as we had only brought smaller versions with us. My intention had been to use Mepps lures in sizes 1 and 2 with a possibility of using size 3 but I was surprised when Huw advocated using sizes 4 and 5. All in all it was a good meeting and I'm sure Huw would have relished joining us had he been able to put his foot to the floor but it wasn't going to be possible on this occasion. We didn't forget to obtain the directions for the boathouse and the key for the padlock that secured the boats before saying our farewells. On leaving, Huw told us to watch out for the "Lady of Snowdon" and the Peregrine Falcons that frequent the area around the lake. I would certainly keep an eye open to see if I could catch a glimpse of my first

Peregrine but the "Lady of Snowdon" was a bit of a mystery...

The beginning of our free day saw us heading for the Llanberis end of the lake to familiarise ourselves with the location where most of the fishing would take place. As luck would have it, the car park was close to the shoreline, which gave us a bird's eye view of the area. Rawson scanned around with binoculars and soon located the "jigging" marks that consisted of three buoys anchored in close proximity of each other. Tying up the boat to one of these to fish for Arctic Char with maggots was a mouth-watering prospect for me. The lake setting here at the entrance to Llanberis Pass was magnificent with the northern flanks of Mount Snowdon seated majestically in the foreground. Even if the fish didn't feed the following day, we could always just lie back and take in the stunning views all around us from the middle of the lake. We took the opportunity to follow the footpath through Padarn Country Park to get a closer look at the lake. On route I asked a passer-by if he could help us to find the "Lady of Snowdon" and he duly obliged. The mysterious spectacle was in fact a rock formation that resembled a human face. It was clearly visible in the sunshine for all to see between two mountain pinnacles. After taking a couple of photographs we could now cross this one off the list! We continued walking until we reached the point where Llyn Padarn ended and the next lake along the valley, Llyn Peris, began. There didn't seem to be anything further to glean from our ambles so we decided to re-trace our steps back to the car - next stop was Caernarfon...

↓

Can you spot "The Lady of Snowdon"?

Having picked up some necessary bits and pieces from the tackle shop, we wanted to ascertain the fishing potential around Caernarfon Harbour. It was only a short walk away and in hindsight I'm pleased that we had taken the trouble. The inner section of the harbour was huge and there was plenty of space to cast a line. For some reason all the resident boats had been moored at one end but more importantly the place was simply teeming with Mullet in the 3 to 4lb bracket. They certainly looked an easy target as they cruised around nonchalantly in the sunshine. There was a big problem though - it was a long way up from the water and there were no access points or steps to land any fish hooked. A drop-net seemed to be the only solution but we didn't have one with us on this occasion. In any case time was at a premium so we were unable to exploit the opportunity but it was something to keep on the backburner until a later date. Without further ado it was off to Cwellyn to collect the electric engine, battery and of course our permits for the following two days. There were no problems encountered here but when we returned to the caravan it was a different story. Since arriving, the weather had remained very hot indeed and I had become paranoid about the welfare of our precious supply of maggots. They had been placed in the fridge and I was checking them out at every opportunity. Unfortunately I can only assume that I hadn't replaced the lid correctly on the last occasion because as Rawson opened the caravan door his expression was one of abject horror. I believe he had visions of his wife murdering him when he returned home. The carpeted floor was literally swimming in maggots and it took us hours to pick them out of the pile. Before retiring to bed we re-checked the place was clear but during the night when I got up to answer a call of nature, I found that hundreds had appeared again and it took another hour to extract them from the wiry fabric - just what you need in the middle of the night!!!...

Having already loaded the car the night before with all the tackle and provisions we were able to make a rapid start after the alarm woke us at 5am. We headed directly for the boathouse at Penllyn, which was situated on the banks of the Afon (River) Rhythallt just two minutes drive away. We had the choice of three "Troutfisher" boats which were waiting on stand-by when we pulled in. They looked ideal for the job in hand. Apparently these boats had been designed by a Trout fisherman for Trout fishermen and were purposely built with safety in mind to be rowed or powered by as little as 2hp. Buoyancy was high up around the gunwales where it was needed and with a length of nearly 16 feet there was oodles of space. Our equipment was stored conveniently on board including the oars before we were ready to launch. In view of the prolonged dry spell the river was very low which meant that we had to drag the boat through the shallows for about 30 yards to avoid grounding it on the rocky bottom. The wading only took a matter of minutes and we were soon going through the middle arch of the ancient, picture-postcard stone bridge before entering into the edge of Llyn Padarn. Here the water deepened and we were able to climb aboard. After a couple of punts with the ends of the oars we were ready to begin our adventure into the picturesque lake that stretched out in front of us for about two miles. The scenery was both beautiful and diverse. It ranged from small rocky outcrops to acres of loose scree and steep forestry - a wild habitat perfect for wildlife. Rawson lowered the engine and turned the throttle, sparking life into the boat, which crept along silently through the calm dark waters. Huw's instructions were to begin trolling about three quarters of a mile up the lake where a large promontory came in from the right. From here I believe the depth increased significantly which would give us a better chance of coming into contact with a Char. One thing was for sure - it was going to be a long day so we had to be economical with the engine to prevent the battery from running flat. While Rawson acted as pilot, I pieced the rods together so they would be ready at the appropriate time. For the record, Rawson's lure was a Mepps number 3 (Comet) with blue spots and mine was a Mepps number 5 (Comet) with red spots. After a few minutes we were passing the terminus of the Llanberis Lake Railway at Penllyn. The little steam locomotives in their highly polished and coloured livery are certainly a reminder of days gone by. I couldn't wait to get to the prime position further up the lake so we did a "spinner" test early, alternating the throttle speed in order to determine the optimum setting to operate the boat. Huw had told us to troll at the slowest speed possible but making sure that the spinner was working consistently, and that turned out to be number two on the throttle control. The lures were cast about 40 yards off the stern and the two rods were positioned so they stuck out at right angles from each side of the boat. As confirmation that all was well, the rod tips were nodding their approval as the blades of the spinners rotated unfalteringly down in the depths. For the record, our main lines were 6lb breaking strain and the six foot traces from the leads were 5lb. Now and then the rod tips kicked as the lures hit bottom and it was necessary to retrieve them to clear the debris that had accumulated on the blades and treble hooks. We could have lightened the leads to avoid this happening but we weren't too far from the deeper water so stuck with it for the time being. There had been no sign of the Peregrine but it was some consolation to have seen a couple of Dabchicks.

"Troutfisher" boats at Penllyn

Travelling at slow speed on a large lake gave the impression that we weren't moving at all but of course this was just an illusion - in fact we were fast approaching the wider part of the lake where our chances of catching would be improved. The time arrived when we could start zig-zagging across the lake, enabling us to cover as much water as possible with the lures. My eyes were switching from one rod tip to the other, willing one of them to get a take, but every time it was just the usual rhythmic tapping as the spinner's blades revolved unhindered. The angle of the lines showed that the lures were working deep down but I was glad that now there were no instances of them snagging or touching bottom in the deeper water. We continued for a couple of hours working slowly up the lake, going over the likely looking spots twice until reaching the bay at the far end - it was here that my luck changed. As Rawson got the boat ready to turn around to go back down the lake, I began to retrieve the lines to check that the lures were clear of particles of weed etc. During the recovery of the lure on the second rod, a fish took the spinner as I brought it up from the depths through the shallower layers. My heart was pounding in anticipation but not nearly as fast as the fish at the end of the line, which was certainly giving a good account of itself. A couple more turns on the reel and the fish broke surface a few yards from the boat where I could clearly see it was a Char, but then disaster struck. The fish shook itself free from the Mepps number 5 before there was a chance to net it and I was inwardly distraught. Strangely though, I was able to quickly cast aside the negative inclinations because I felt that it would only be a matter of time before another hook-up occurred. However, as the hours passed by without incident, my confidence waned and I couldn't avoid turning my attention to the disappointment of the near miss - it was time to try some maggot fishing.

Fortunately there were no other fishing boats tied up to the buoys so we had the place to ourselves. For added stability we attached our boat at both ends using two of the buoys before altering our seating positions, allowing us to fish comfortably off the side of the boat. Plumbing the depth I estimated that we had about 60 feet below the boat and I couldn't wait to drop my rig down to the target zone. This would seem an opportune time to mention that the controlling Angling Society does not allow groundbaiting or the introduction of maggots prior to or during fishing sessions, which includes the use of bait-droppers and swimfeeders. Such a ruling on a game fishery is quite understandable but it was frustrating to think that we had to find the fish on this large expanse of water without any free offerings - a somewhat daunting task. Anyway, for the record our paternoster leger rigs consisted of a couple of six inch hook links of 2½lb breaking strain line which were finished off with size 14 hooks. A one ounce lead held the rig in position so the bottom hook fluttered six inches off the bottom and the higher one about 18 inches. For added attraction I could jig the rig to give the maggots some movement if the mood so took me but my focus was really to present a static bait and watch the quiver tip for any bites. Both leads were lowered to the floor of the lake before the lines were tightened appropriately so the leads were just touching bottom. Everything was ready and my eyes didn't stray from the quiver that was moving rhythmically with the slight rocking of the boat. Nothing stirred for the first hour but then the quiver tip on my rod juddered and pulled downwards before springing back to the normal position. Instinctively my hands moved to grip the rod as the quiver pulled over for a second time and I struck but unfortunately didn't connect with the fish. I reeled up and changed the baits immediately before re-settling the rig but the bite was not repeated - in fact the rod tips remained unmoved for the duration. It should be noted that I also tried jigging the tackle close to the bottom but my rigs just tangled badly every time so a re-think was definitely necessary. On the way back to Penllyn the trolling rods were employed once again so no fishing time was wasted, but this unfortunately was also to no avail. Oh how I wished I had boated the Char hooked earlier that morning.

Rawson — life before the oars!

throughout Padarn Country Park at that time of the year. The sun was now fiercer than ever and by the time we arrived at the buoys poor old Rawson needed a break and some urgent liquid refreshment. As his spent, sweaty body slumped into the bottom of the boat, he reminded me of Charlton Heston playing the part of a slave in the biblical epic, Ben Hur. One particular scene showed the film star shackled in chains in the galley of a Roman ship and, you may remember, the slaves were continually flogged as they heaved away on the oars to the beat of a drum in the stifling heat. In fact Rawson looked to be in his final death throes and I was tempted to revive him with a bucket of cool lake water but changed my mind because I didn't want to scare the fish!

Anchored up ready for some "jigging"

Anyway, the boat was anchored to just one of the buoys this time. In effect this would mean that the boat would be subject to a little more movement, allowing us to cover extra ground with our jigged maggots. It was hot work though and it got harder as the day continued. Flicking the wrist deftly and reeling slowly in a rhythmic sequence for a few hours to try to attract the Char is tiring enough but especially so when the fish are not playing ball. Maybe it was our technique, maybe it was the bright sun or maybe the fish didn't pass through our zone - the answer was anyone's guess. I felt sure that had the Char come into contact with the bait they would have accepted it readily because the end-tackle was fine and tied painstakingly to perfection - and it's not as if these fish can be hook-shy. Nevertheless, we fished on regardless until evening before heading back to Penllyn. Rawson took to the oars again and the lures were employed for the last time but there were no takes and my mind reverted back to the "one that got away". The mission had failed but it had been fun and I had learned a lot - I would have to make time and try again another day.

For those of you who, like myself, are inclined to catch this species you will find that there are plenty of pointers as well as a number of do's and don'ts contained in this chapter. Despite the fact that I was unsuccessful with my quest, interested parties can certainly learn by my mistakes and take advantage of the wealth of information incorporated here.

+++++

After all the trials and tribulations it was very disappointing that my efforts had been in vain but I had a feeling deep down that this result was on the cards. Having given the

Cumbrian Lakes my best shot and subsequently failing to pick up a Welsh Char, perhaps I should now look towards Scotland to achieve my goal. Alternatively it looks like I shall have to don the Arctic survival kit and a suitable drill for a spell of ice fishing in Scandinavia or the like - watch this space!!!

Chapter X

Beyond Reasonable Doubt (06.05.2006)

I'm pretty sure that I have caught Silver Bream in the past but the problem is I cannot be certain of the fact. Identification of these fish has never been a straightforward exercise and during latter years has become further confused with hybridisation. It's frustrating though, because I still have vivid memories of fishing at Twickenham Pit, near Waltham Cross in Hertfordshire, and catching small Bream which possessed all the usual characteristics of the Silver variety. These fish had fins tinged with red and the large eye that is typical of the species and were recorded as such in my fishing register. However, in view of the element of doubt regarding their true identity, the original entries made in the log during the mid 1960's have now been revised and as a consequence the Silver Bream has come back onto my target list.

In my eyes there was only one choice of venue where the objective could be realised conclusively and that was the Mill Farm Fishery near Pulborough in West Sussex. Here, numbers of these rare fish are caught on a regular basis and the added bonus is that there is always a possibility of catching a record breaker at the same time. In fact, there have been a string of British record "Blicca bjoerkna" captured at Mill Farm and at the time of writing I believe there is a claim pending for a fish weighing in excess of 2lbs for the first time. Nevertheless, before making the 300 mile round journey I thought I'd ring the Head Bailiff, Adrian Brown to get the "gen" on the fishery and try to establish my chances of connecting with a Silver. It transpired that my best opportunity was to make a visit before the hot weather set in, so I opted for a day during the early part of May. Furthermore, I was told that a red maggot approach using a waggler or the pole was producing the majority of captures, with worms and breadflake sometimes taking the better fish.

Apparently the fishery has a close season imposed between New Years Day and Good Friday in order to safeguard the habitat and ensure the fish are not over-pressured. In my opinion this "rest" policy makes sound sense as I would imagine that the relatively small pool receives a great deal of attention from specimen hunters coming from far afield to try their luck for a new record. It appears that the fishery had been developed in the heart of the countryside on ground that was previously grassland. With conservation in mind, the concept was to create a pool amidst a natural, wooded environment which would attract wildlife and anglers alike. The pool is both spacious and attractive, affording plenty of bankside cover along with seductive bays and an island. It incorporates 40 natural pegs and the depth ranges from between two and seven feet. The bottom is smooth and bowl shaped and doesn't contain any notable holes as such, which in theory means that anglers have an even chance of success wherever they choose to set up their stools. Apart from the Silver Bream the three-acre pool holds a good head of Carp, Perch, Roach, Tench and Crucians, which have attained a decent size and should provide extremely good sport on the float - just what the doctor ordered.

I made arrangements with Richard Fobbester to join me on this little escapade to West Sussex. At the time, Richard had been busy plundering big slabs at Nazeing Meads but welcomed the chance to bag a true Silver Bream, which would finally put the identification muddle to bed. Not being big fans of the pole, we opted for a waggler approach just in case any big fish intercepted the bait. Our poles are certainly not specialised and it was felt that a good fish hooked is less likely to be lost with rod and reel. This decision was reinforced by the fact that both of us are undoubtedly more accustomed to the rod and certainly a lot more comfortable playing fish to the net with one. The rods were set up in advance and tucked away in the quiver bags so no time would be wasted on site. For the record, the tackle on my main rod consisted of a 2lb breaking strain main line, a customised insert waggler with bristle and a size 14 hook (Kamasan B520) tied to a 1¾lb link - now we were ready to rock 'n' roll...

Despite the early morning start, the traffic was busy on the M25 approaching the Dartford Tunnel, but at least it kept moving. To all intents and purposes the journey had been straight forward enough, assisted by the autoroute printout that had steered us inexorably towards our destination at Watersfield, just off the A29 Bognor Road. Motoring through the surrounding villages and the rural landscape on the last part of our trek had been very pleasurable - the area was a typical reflection of old England at it's best. It was 6.15am when we entered the fishery where it soon became evident that we hadn't been the first to arrive. The waters had already been opened for business prior to the advertised opening time of 7am, which meant that we needed to crack on without delay. With the adrenalin now pumping, we unloaded the gear and set off at a clip to locate our objective. It was a fine morning with clear blue skies and not a whisper of wind, although heavy rain had been forecast. Our route initially took us past the Hammer Pool and the fishermen's hut before we reached the delectable Mill Pool. It was every bit as attractive as it had been described and as such our spirits were raised a further couple of notches. The water was calm and coloured and our immediate impression was that the lake contained a large head of fish and that they were feeding avidly throughout. It was also apparent that the Carp had begun their spawning ritual, which may have also attributed to the profound colour of the water. The Carp were crashing about in the usual frenzied state at various spots all round the lake and seemed oblivious to the presence of the other anglers. We felt that the preoccupation was certainly good news for us as the Carp would be unlikely to want our bait. Whilst it can be great fun catching Carp on light tackle, in these circumstances it could be looked upon as a hindrance at the expense of our main target, the Silver Bream. An interruption of this kind would not only absorb valuable time in trying to land the fish but also in allowing the swim to recover after the resulting disturbance.

Making our way towards the far-end of the pool we came upon a couple of inviting pegs close to the island. There was a bit of fish movement there and I couldn't wait to make the first cast, but first I needed to make a slight adjustment to my rig. We had heard that the Bream were being caught more or less under the rod tip so I thought I could get away with something a little lighter than my insert waggler. I selected a pole float carrying 5 x No.6 shot and in hindsight was glad I'd taken the trouble to make the change. The new outfit was better suited to the conditions and as a result I believe both bite and catch rates were improved. With each cast I was loose-feeding hempseed, corn and maggots in order to stimulate the fish into action, and began the day using double red maggot on the hook. The first few casts produced small Roach before I latched on to a Carp that took several minutes to subdue - so much for the Carp not feeding! After this the bites slowed as I had expected, although it didn't take too long for the Roach to oblige once again. Richard had started in similar fashion, catching Roach, but out of the blue he suddenly landed the perfect Silver Bream weighing about 6ozs. This was just what we had been hoping for and we studied it's anatomy with interest before it was returned - bravo Dick! In fact his next six fish were all Silvers and the rib-pulling started up in earnest as I hadn't yet had a sniff of one. A shoal had obviously moved on to his feed and I prayed that they were going to spread across into my little zone.

Bream can sometimes be suckers for worms so I changed the bait to a Dendrobaena and had quickly caught two nice Crucians, which were just over the pound mark, when the Bailiff arrived. We had already spoken at length on the telephone but as they say there is no substitute for meeting someone in the flesh. It always pays to invest a little time talking to the experts, especially on a first time visit to a fishery. I really wanted to know the origins of this rare breed of fish but with everything else that was going on, I forgot to ask. We did learn however, that the fish normally go off the feed by noon and don't turn on again until about 4pm. This meant that within our own timescale we only had a further three or four hours of good fishing left. The Bailiff was adamant that we should move into the hot pegs that had recently been producing plenty of quality Silver Bream, which were situated about 30 yards away. He was surprised that they were still vacant so we needed to move quickly, but before we had time to react, Richard's float slid away and he struck into a better fish. After a brief tussle the fish was netted safely - it was a beautiful specimen Silver Bream that weighed 1lb 5ozs. We really hadn't expected to catch fish of this calibre on our first attempt, especially within the first hour of arriving. The Bailiff, who must have witnessed a similar scenario many times before, bade us farewell as the cameras came out to capture the moment. We were very grateful for the inside information that he had given us, which we had every intention of exploiting to the full of course. To think that it wasn't so long ago that the British record stood at less than a pound, it suddenly registered how privileged we were to be able to fish on such a distinguished water for the price of a day ticket. Without further ado the equipment was quickly transferred back to the recommended pegs that had fortunately remained unoccupied...

The rain was now coming down in stair-rods but within minutes of settling into my new surroundings, my float buried and I found myself attached to my first Silver Bream, which weighed 11ozs. To put it mildly, I was overjoyed and somewhat relieved to have caught one of these scarce fish at long last. The new pitch had certainly not disappointed and the fishing resumed apace, with bites occurring within seconds of the bait settling on the bottom. In fact, the non-stop action continued until about 12.30pm when the fish seemed to switch off, giving us time to relax and discuss our achievements. The light tackle sport had been remarkable during the relatively short session and much better than we had anticipated. The only downside had been the continual interference of the Carp, which had kept me tied down for considerable periods throughout the morning. I would estimate that half my fishing time was spent playing these warriors when I could have been concentrating on the more timid Silvers. I'm sure that without the unceasing commotion the chance of catching a fish nearing 2lbs is always a possibility! I must really try and make time to return to this idyllic, well-kept fishery sometime with a view to extracting one of the biggies. In the meantime our statistics for the day were as follows:

Richard: 26 Silver Bream, six over a pound, best 1lb 5ozs

Me: 19 Silver Bream, three over a pound, best 1lb 4½ozs

Apart from the Silver Bream, which averaged 12ozs, we accounted for Crucians up to 2lb, Roach to 1½lb, Common Carp to 8lb, Mirror Carp to 5lb and a smattering of small Tench and Perch.

For me it was reassuring to have cracked this long-standing target that had been eating away at my subconscious for years. The capture didn't only put the matter of identification beyond reasonable doubt, it made it a cast iron certainty, which meant that the Silver Bream issue could be laid to rest once and for all.

Richard's largest authenticated Silver Bream — 1lb 5ozs

Chapter XI

Black Country Bliss (30.10.2006)

I'm always looking to add to my ever-growing angling library so was very happy when one particular book I'd been seeking for a while appeared on an Internet auction site recently.   I was equally pleased when my winning bid secured the book, which was by John Etherington.   The surprise was that the seller turned out to be an old acquaintance, Phil Goodsell, whom I'd joined on a guided fishing holiday in Spain a few years previously.   As I recall, Phil landed his first 100lb Wels Catfish on that notable trip as well as some hefty Carp.   We certainly had a good crack in the searing heat and I shall never forget our escape from the firestorm (see Carpin'On).   We had a long chat to catch up with all the news before he enquired whether I would like the chance to catch a 2lb Roach.   Well, putting such a proposition to me was like asking if the Pope was a Catholic — you bet I did!   I've rarely targeted big Roach specifically and haven't achieved the magical 2lb barrier yet, but would cherish the opportunity to do so.   Over the years I have caught some upper ones, mainly while fishing for other species, but to date a two-pounder has proved elusive.   Phil said these fish were reasonably abundant in a still water that I apparently already knew well as I'd written about it in my previous book.   The venue turned out to be one of my favourite old haunts, the Great Lake situated in the grounds of Himley Hall near Wolverhampton.   In fact I caught my first Grass Carp there some years ago but haven't returned since.   I've always regarded this venue as a Carp fishery although, casting my mind back, I do remember catching a few unexpected Redfins using hair-rigged tiger nuts.

Checking our diaries, we made arrangements to meet up for

a session at the end of October, hoping that by then the Tench would have stopped feeding. Phil sent me a couple of his special rigs that he uses to catch the long-range Roach in advance of our trip so that no time would be lost on the day. The rig (see diagram below) incorporated a weighted maggot feeder and a pair of size 20 hooks tied to three-inch hook links attached via swivels to an 18-inch length of 15lb powergum (hook links are 2lb breaking strain). For all intents and purposes the set up is a form of bolt rig so on no account should bites be struck. The elasticity of the powergum would in some way cushion the impact of a good fish hooking up but, that said, if the Tench start to home in on the bait they'll make short work of the short hook links and we'll be forever re-tackling. Anyway, I made up a couple of extra rigs myself and was looking forward to testing their effectiveness on the day.

Roach Rig

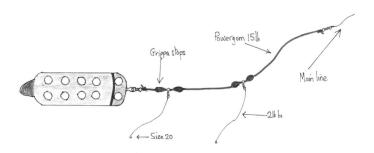

Having allowed myself an hour to make the 45-mile journey, I was pleased when I arrived with time to spare. Phil was already waiting for me at the fishermen's entrance, having opened the combination padlock so it was just a matter of driving straight in. The setting was lovely and as I remembered it — a mixture of rolling pastures mingled with an assortment of large deciduous trees and wooded groves surrounding the Great Lake. Himley Hall actually stands in 180 acres of landscaped parkland that was designed by the famous Lancelot "Capability" Brown. For the record, the place has received regular Royal patronage over the years, including Edward VIII who spent his last weekend there before his abdication, and the Duke and Duchess of Kent who honeymooned there in 1934. I hope they had time to cast a line between their Royal duties! We parked the cars and made our way through the copse towards the dam-side of the lake. Phil's favourite pegs, sited between two trees about 40 yards apart, were fortunately vacant and in a part of the 16 acre pool I hadn't fished before. Looking across the calm waters of the lake in the early morning was what fishing is all about. Coots and Grebes were frolicking and there was a gathering of nomadic horses drinking at the waterside on the opposite bank. There was also a lot of fish activity, with boils and rolls popping up all over the place. Had we been Carp or Tench fishing I'm sure we would have scored, despite the fact that it was mid-autumn. The barometer reading before I left home was 1010mb which I hoped would suit the Roach. An average temperature of 15°c was forecast with moderate south-westerly winds — positively balmy for that time of the year.

My choice of rods was a pair of 11 foot, 1¾lb test curve specialist Bream rods that had been built by John Wilson in the late 1980's for the purpose of our Irish Bream exploits. These faithful servants have got a lovely "soft" action throughout and would be just the job for both casting the distance and playing fish on the light hook links. I married the rods up with a couple of Shimano 5010 GT reels that had been loaded with 5lb Maxima, before setting the clutches carefully. Bait for the day was two pints of maggots with equal quantities of whites and reds. First job was to introduce a little bait via the feeders into the target zone about 50 yards out before the tiny hooks were baited with a single maggot. The casts were made and I sat back to await developments and I didn't have to wait too long. Within minutes the swingers were flashing up and down as fish attacked the baits and I was riveted with anticipation. Soon enough there was a hook-up and I found myself guiding a fish carefully to the waiting net. The first fish weighed about half a pound or so and was in pristine condition. Early sport was certainly hectic and there were times when I had to dispense with one of the rods because the bites were coming so quickly. Phil was bang-on the money though with a string of big Roach coming to the net together with a smattering of agile Tench. Just before noon my indicator rose and I leaned into something more substantial — this was no Roach. After some anxious moments and a few minutes of coaxing, the fish was beaten and I netted a Pike weighing about 7lbs. This was a turn up for the book — a Pike on a single maggot hooked cleanly in the scissors. The sport continued and by the end of the day (gates were closing at 5pm) I had landed between 30 and 40 prime Roach to 1lb 12ozs — not bad for a first attempt. The average size of the Roach I had caught was about 10ozs whereas Phil's average fish was probably over the pound mark. In fact Phil's tally included a dozen Roach over a pound with the best of them going 1lb 14ozs, 1lb 15ozs and 2lb 1oz. He had achieved yet another Roach from this super venue above the magical 2lb barrier as well as landing some hefty Tench. This was impressive stuff from the day ticket fishery and I couldn't wait to have another crack for a 2lb fish myself...

Two days later (01.11.2006)

At the crack of dawn I found myself setting up my

equipment again at a peg positioned between where Phil and I had fished previously. Unfortunately however the first bout of frost of the year had occurred overnight and temperatures had plummeted by more than 10 degrees to 2°c. There was also a biting northerly breeze blowing into my face and my hands were numb before I had started. A degree in engineering is required to work out the assembly of my old stainless steel pod under normal circumstances but with cold mitts it was even more of a nightmare. Anyway, I managed to fumble my way through and soon had everything in place ready to go. The reels were already "clipped up" from the previous session so it was just a matter of baiting and wanging out the feeders to the required distance. Previously, the alarms had been bleeping with fish activity within minutes but on this occasion they remained silent. It quickly became evident that the cold snap had put the fish down and I had to hope that I would be able to switch them back on again. I kept the bait flowing every 10 minutes or so but still there was no sign of a fish. The monotony was broken for a while when a group of "twitchers" arrived with their high-tech equipment to see a rare visitor to the pool. It was a solitary Ruddy Duck that was scooting and diving all over the place in the central area of the lake. The audience appeared to be well impressed with the performance of the hen bird doing its stuff a 100 yards from the shore. I understand that Ruddy Ducks were once commonplace in this country but sadly they are now as rare as rocking horse dung. Anyway, after four hours of non-activity I was feeling somewhat chilled and dejected when out of the blue the indicator slammed up tight to the rod. It was a big relief when I leaned into my first fish of the day, which at first I thought was a Tench. However, as matters progressed the nodding and jagging told me that the fish was more than likely a Roach. As I guided the fish gradually back to my position I caught a glimpse of red fins as it surfaced and I prayed that the tiny hook would hold firm. Slowly but surely I brought it under control before easing it over the frame of the net — she was mine. Looking down at the handsome specimen in the mesh I immediately knew it was a personal best and also that it was going to be more than 2lbs! I don't know why but suddenly my demeanour changed from one of despondency to one of pure bliss. The scales were zeroed with the weigh sling before I held the fish aloft and scrutinised the reading on the Avon's dial — 2lb 6ozs, absolutely fantastic! To know that this important milestone had at last been achieved was very gratifying indeed. My spirits had been raised with all the activity that had warmed the blood and I was raring to try for another. During the following two hours I managed to bank a further 10 Roach to 1lb 10ozs together with a solitary 2lb plus Crucian before packing up and heading for home. To use an old Black Country expression, the fishing here could be described as "bostin" which I understand means excellent — the day certainly went well for me, apart from the shadowy photograph of my fish that wasn't up to standard for the book.

The rumours are that Carp anglers have encountered Roach above the 3lbs mark at Himley, which is extremely encouraging. From my limited experience it would appear that big Roach are prolific in the water, probably thriving on the volume of high protein bait that has been introduced over the years. In my view there is every possibility of picking up one of these giants here, particularly during the winter months, and the place will definitely be receiving a lot of my attention in the future.

Phil with his best fish of the day — 2lb 1oz

Chapter XII

Holiday Capers

I've had a great deal of success hunting different species whilst on holiday, although keeping the rest of the family content at the same time can sometimes be a little difficult. In order to maintain the status quo, I have to limit my fishing time so as not to interfere too much with the flow of normal holiday routines. My aim is to be as co-operative as possible in all aspects in order to avoid my wife coming out with that old hackneyed phrase "This isn't a fishing holiday you know!" Another negative factor is that I am unable to use my usual array of tackle and have to make do with a telescopic rod, which is far from ideal. At least it's gratifying to know that some tackle manufacturers have now recognised the market for the travelling angler. There is definitely a far greater choice in the shops today and the quality of the products is much improved. In fact I have recently purchased a very nice six-piece carbon match rod made by Flaven that fits comfortably into my suitcase. The protective container is tough enough to withstand the rigours of modern air travel including the normal harsh treatment meted out by the flight baggage handlers. For me, fishing during family holidays boils down to a matter of being prepared and seizing the opportunity as and when it arises.

Half the battle is winning over the wife and mine deserves a medal. She suffers badly under my constant references to fishing but I've got to know the boundaries of tolerance and I must say that a happy balance is generally achieved. Another testing time can be when my wife is about to actually make a booking for the holiday. If the glossy brochures show no evidence of somewhere to cast a line, like a quaint harbour or a juicy river, then I have to use all my charm and a lot of diplomacy to persuade her to look elsewhere - I have to accept that my passion for a fishing challenge can go a little too far sometimes.

Sneaking in a holiday fishing session here and there is all well and good as long as bait has been catered for. Obtaining bait in a foreign country can sometimes be a problem but I don't despair because there is always bread to fall back on. To be on the safe side, my ploy is to tuck away a pint of maggots and a tub of brandling worms in the suitcase, which takes care of any freshwater opportunity that may arise. Things don't always go according to plan though - once I took a pint of maggots to the Greek Islands with a view to hammering the Mullet. Arriving at the hotel I placed the maggots, which had survived the flight, into the fridge. A couple of days later I packed them in my rucksack to take them by boat to a place named Lindos for a first bout of fishing. As the boat entered the bay the stifling heat was incredible - Lindos must be the hottest place on Earth. After the boat had berthed my son Lee and I wandered off to look for a good Mulleting hole, which really was just a formality in Greek waters. I assembled the tackle on the telescopic rod before removing the bait box from my bag to check the health of the maggots. I found them to be in first-rate order but within a matter of seconds of being exposed to the ferocious heat they had become stretched and lifeless. In fact they had died in front of my eyes and all the trouble and care that I had gone to, to ensure their freshness, had been wasted - which meant that there was no fishing on that day!

As far as I am concerned the holiday "chance" sessions are simply a means to an end and only act to complement the rest of my angling activities. They are in no way organised to replace serious fishing breaks and specialist guided arrangements that are the mainstay of my fishing programme. Anyway, to provide a little flavour of my holiday capers overseas I have written a few brief accounts as follows:

+++++

<u>Lake Garda, Italy (20.08.2004)</u>

My wife and I were about to board a ferry in the beautiful town of Riva on the shores of Lake Garda when I noticed something very interesting. Displayed on the wall of the ferry-station was an information poster showing the different species of fish that inhabit the lake. The names were written in Italian but I recognised all the pictures, but with one exception. I was thrilled because here was a prospect of catching a new freshwater species and that's a relatively rare occurrence these days. The fish in question closely resembles a Roach although there is a dark band that stretches along the lateral line. The Italian name for the fish is Triotto (Rutilus aula.) This fish, which only grows to a maximum length of eight inches, is endemic to Italy and in particular to the lakes of Padua in the Venetian region in the north of the country...

After a couple of days of acclimatisation, I took a stroll along the shore where I found a secluded spot that was suitable to cast a line, just on the outskirts of a little harbour at Porto San Nicolo. The water here was crystal clear and shelved sharply into vast depths so it was a case of presenting a bait on the steep shelf under the rod tip in about 10 feet of water. My float tackle consisted of a Drennan insert waggler carrying shot equivalent to 2AA and a size 20 hook tied to a 1.7lb link - bait was a single maggot. After loose-feeding the swim at intervals for about 20 minutes the first bite came and I found myself attached to a Chub that fought hard on the light tackle. Without a landing net I had to play the 2lb fish for a while before it could be beached safely. The second bite produced a smaller fish that I had been hoping to catch - a Triotto. Its flanks had a yellowish tinge and the tell-tale dark band that I had seen on the identification poster was clearly present - job done!

+++++

Mandraki Harbour, Greece (27.08.1994)

Making our way by taxi from our hotel in Ixia, I had the idea of fishing in Mandraki Harbour while my wife and daughter went shopping. The deep-water venue is situated in the ancient town of Rhodes in the Aegean Sea. Fortunately I had found a shop selling ragworms, which was a real bonus, although I had brought plenty of bread in reserve for the ever-obliging Mullet. On arrival I threw in a couple of handfuls of mashed bread to get the fish in feeding mood and almost immediately, the surface of the water literally erupted as thousands of fingerling Mullet competed for the free offerings. Using light float tackle I began catching these finicky biting fish before changing the bait to ragworm. By now a crowd of on-lookers had gathered for the show and Lee captured the event using a video camera, ridiculing me with his commentary in the process – swine! Anyway, I increased the float depth to the maximum that I could handle comfortably with the 10-foot telescopic rod before dropping the bait close to the harbour wall. Within a couple of minutes the float slid away and up came a handsome Rainbow Wrasse, which was a first for me. Presenting the bait close to the bottom meant that bites were more difficult to come by but I persevered and came up trumps with another new species before it was time to leave. The fish was a Bogue, which I believe is a member of the Sea Bream family and has been known to turn up in

British waters on occasion. The following day I decided to take a rod down to the beach at Ixia in order to use the remaining ragworms, while the rest of the clan relaxed in the turquoise sea. Casting into open water from a pebbly beach that stretched for miles seemed a bit of a tall order but surprisingly I didn't have to wait long before my rod registered a bite. In fact bites continued unabated even when the other three members of my family were fighting for dominance of an airbed that was floating directly above my bait in four feet of water! After 20 minutes the bait had been exhausted but during that period I did manage to land two different varieties of Sea Bream. These fish were unidentified at the time so it was important that I took some photographic evidence for the record. Fortunately at a later date I was able to make a positive identification of both species from a book by Ioannis Batjakas and Alistair Economakis. This super little reference book entitled "Coastal Fishes of Greece" was just ideal for my activities. The Bream in question turned out to be the "Striped" and the "Two Banded" varieties.

+++++

Seagull Pier, Gambia (08.03.1993)

During a holiday treat in the Gambia to celebrate our wives 40th birthdays, Richard Fobbester and I took a couple of hours out to cast a line. Leaving the girls sunning themselves by the pool at the Atlantic Hotel, we summoned the services of a guide to help us find a suitable spot to fish. First job was to obtain some Bonga Fish for bait so we set off for the market in the heart of Banjul Town. The place was a hive of activity and wandering through the jam-packed aisles in the market turned out to be a real ordeal for me. It was very hot, very dusty and very smelly and I was tagging along retching all the way towards the fishmonger's pitch. The last straw came as we passed the butcher's stall where I was physically sick on the move as we picked our way through the crowds. I had caught sight of a large Camel's head that had flies emanating from every orifice and the stench in the midday sun was appalling. The people around me jumped out of the way shouting as I threw up and in the turmoil I lost contact with my colleagues, who were unaware of my distress. I had to quickly pull myself together, overcome the embarrassment and set about finding the other pair among the maze of stalls. Fortunately my chosen route through the throng was the correct one and I soon located them, bartering with the fish merchant. With bait organised we headed off to Seagull Pier for our short fishing session. The area surrounding the pier was under building construction and our guide Dan, advised us that we would need permission to access the site, before leaving to negotiate with the builders. It wasn't long before he returned with a broad smile on his face, having been given the green light without the need to oil anyone's palm, so it was cheers all round. The sea looked relatively shallow and our aim was to cast as far as possible with our Carp rods. The size 6 hooks were baited with a small chunk of Bonga Fish before the two-ounce leads were launched into the soupy water. For the record I understand that Bonga Fish is the Gambian name for the Allis Shad, a fish that once thrived in both the River Shannon and River Severn but sadly, for one reason or another, have now declined. That's definitely not the case in the Gambia though, as huge numbers are netted for local consumption. Most of these fish are landed by canoe at a place named Tanji, where they are washed and taken to the smoking houses for curing. During a safari a couple of days earlier we had actually been shown around the sheds to see the smoking process and sample the end product for ourselves. I was a little wary of trying it at first because of past experience of eating Shad but this was delicious - the flesh of the fish just fell away from the bones. Visiting the fishing community at Tanji that day was the highlight of the tour for me and the memory will always remain imprinted in my mind.

Anyway, getting back to the action - within minutes of casting, Richard's rod was tapping and he reeled in a Sompat Grunt and I followed suit with another soon after. We had already encountered this species on an earlier session at the Denton Bridge and, as before, Dan's family were going to be the beneficiaries.   Next fish went to Richard - it was a Biglip Grunt that weighed about a pound. After a quiet period, my rod began to nod again and this time I landed an African Threadfin also known as a Captain Fish. This species had been our top target in Gambia and we had been looking forward to witnessing the characteristic transparent nose of this splendid fish. Despite the fact that Threadfins can grow to monstrous proportions, I was delighted with my capture even though it weighed less than 2lbs. In the remaining time available to us we were unable to connect with any more of these fish which was a shame for Richard but that's how the cookie crumbles sometimes. The last fish to be landed was a Prickly Pufferfish, which was another first for me and was a fitting end to our West African experience.

+++++

River Arno, Italy (27.08.2005)

My wife and I arrived in Pisa for a few days sight-seeing, but it wasn't the Leaning Tower that I wanted to view first, it was the river that bisected the town. Taking a peek over the bridge (Ponti Di Mezzo) into the margins of the River Arno I could see numbers of nice-sized Mullet, but curiously there were no anglers as far as the eye could see. The following morning, as we walked across the bridge again to catch the bus, I paused to throw some bread into the area where I had seen the fish previously. It wasn't long before four bread rolls had been gorged by a variety of species competing for the surface offerings. Big Roach, Mullet, Chub, Mirror Carp and even Wels Catfish were all sucking in chunks of bread crust that were drifting slowly downstream with the current. The fish were a decent size as well and would certainly have made easy pickings. This was a very exciting development so we decided to call into the Tourist Information Office to make some enquiries about the necessary fishing permits. Unfortunately the news was disappointing - I was told that I would require written approval in advance from the authorities, which usually takes several weeks to finalise. The times I've been thwarted by needless bureaucracy are now getting beyond a joke and I was gutted by the disclosure. However, they did throw me a lifeline. Apparently the local fishermen gather at a place named Marina Di Pisa, which was about 10 miles downstream, where the River Arno empties into the Ligurean Sea. We were further informed that the Livorno bus stops there every hour and the journey takes about half an hour. I would be unlikely to catch the freshwater species seen earlier but at least I should be able to wet a line - this was just what I had been hoping for...

A couple of days later we bought the bus tickets and lined up to take our turn at the "fermata dell autobus" ready for our journey to Marina Di Pisa. The route followed the course of the River Arno, which seemed to grow a little wider as we progressed towards our destination. For the first few miles the reed-lined waterway was virtually uninhabited but as we got closer to the sea it became increasingly busy. It wasn't long before we spotted the section occupied by rows of anglers just on the edge of town so we stopped the bus to get off. Making our way back to where the fishermen were operating, we found that most of the bank space, which stretched for about a 100 yards or so, was already taken. There was very little room to manoeuvre, but luckily a couple of guys fishing on a small wooden jetty invited me to join them. The view upstream was a continuous line of little fishing huts, boathouses and huge contraptions used for netting shoals of passing fish. The large wooden-framed nets, measuring about five yards square, were lowered into the water and left for about half an hour before being levered up again. It was interesting to watch the catch of tiny fish being bounced into the centre of the net where they were readied for transfer to the fish-box. What they did with a catch of such tiny fish was a mystery but I surmised that they were used to make fish broth or the like. Anyway, the water had a nice brown tinge to it and the bottom was made up of mud and fine sand which was an ideal environment for Sole or perhaps Weever - fish high on my target list. It was therefore a little bit of a surprise to me that all the anglers were using long poles and ultra light float tackle to catch Sea Bream. In the limited time available to me I could only follow suit but realised that I was going to struggle with my rather clumsy telescopic outfit. However, I set it up in the best way possible, using the smallest float in my box and a size 20 hook that I baited with a single tentacle of a calamari squid. Fishing was hard on the fast-falling tide and the bites were very tentative. I was trickling my bait along the bottom with the pull of the tide in about four feet of water close to the bank and after 20 minutes without a proper strike, it looked like I was going to fail. Nevertheless, just when I was ready to admit defeat, the float sailed under and I caught a small Annular Sea Bream to add to my growing record listing. This catch was quickly followed by a second bite that produced a stunning fish that turned out to be a Peacock Blenny - it was another first and I was delighted to have scored under such difficult circumstances.

+++++

River Vilaine, France (27.08.1991)

Whilst visiting Pénestin in the Morbihan district of Western France, the challenge was to find a place to fish for the Black Bullhead Catfish - a species not resident in UK waters. I made some enquiries about "le Poisson de Chat" and was directed more in hope than anything else to the River Vilaine. By luck, there was a stretch of open water a few miles from our camping site where yachts and pleasure boats were moored randomly at a spot named Barage D'Arzal. There was easy access, parking and plenty of space to fish and the water looked calm and very inviting. This large basin linked to the River Vilaine would be an ideal resting place for fish during times of heavy water. Shoals of fish could enter the marina to escape the torrent and of course the predators wouldn't be too far behind. The large stretch of water would also have its resident fish and I couldn't wait to give it a try - what a super venue!

Lee and I arrived one evening about two hours before dusk and set up our fixed paternoster rigs and size 10 hooks baited with worms. Casting about 40 yards into about 12 feet of water we caught a number of Bream to 3lbs and some juvenile Zander but there had been no sign of the Catfish. However, as the skies darkened and we were contemplating leaving, one of the optonics started to bleep. Fortunately for me it was the bobbin on my rod that was gradually twitching its way to the butt ring. I picked up the rod and struck into some resistance before continuing to recover line. We waited with bated breath for the fish to appear although deep down I had an inkling that the fish was what we had been looking for. Sure enough, out of the gloom my first Black Bullhead Catfish surfaced just in front of us and I beached it unceremoniously. Taking care to avoid the hazardous spine, the fish was weighed in at just shy of a pound - I was chuffed to bits! Considering we hadn't used any feed or groundbait, our catch had been extremely encouraging in the short time we were there.

"I'm not touching it!" Black Bullhead Catfish

A couple of days later we visited a place named La Brière, which reminded me of the wilder areas of the Norfolk Broads. It was a maze of canals and waterways, criss-crossing through a reedy marshland. There were no footpaths as such so we decided to hire a rowing boat to explore the place, which was a paradise for birdlife. Of course I happened to have a rod with me already set up with very light float tackle with a view to catching something for the fishing record. Having rowed about half a mile from the base I came across a nice fishy spot at a wide section of the canal. The boat was pitched onto a bed of weeds, which acted as an anchor and provided a platform of sorts to fish from. All settled in with minimum disturbance, I cast the float towards the far bank, followed it with a handful of maggots and watched intently for developments. It soon became evident that there was a fair bit of predatory activity in the swim, which was very exciting, but no bites came to my single maggot bait during the first ten minutes. Just when the others were getting itchy feet and wanting to move on, the float suddenly buried and I hooked into something I wasn't quite expecting. After a bit of bumping and boring a Pumpkinseed Sunfish weighing about a quarter pound surfaced in front of the boat. It was brought aboard successfully and provided me with another freshwater personal best - what a result, good planning old man!

The little boat trip through this delightful part of the countryside was very enjoyable but unfortunately we hadn't been equipped to deal with the mosquitoes, and they took no prisoners! We were bitten relentlessly and had to return to base early to prevent any further torture. Any prospective visitors to the area are advised to dress appropriately and ensure they take along plenty of insect repellent!!!

Harbours in Sorrento and Amalfi, Italy (25.08.2006)

A busy schedule meant that I could only fit in three whistle-stop fishing sessions of less than an hour each on this sightseeing holiday. We were based in Sorrento in the Compania region of Italy where I discovered there were two venues with fishing potential. My intention was to try each of them as and when time permitted. I had brought some frozen calamari squid from the UK, which I kept in the hotel fridge so that I would be ready for any short-notice eventuality. The deep waters of the Mare Tirreno (Tyrrhenian Sea) in the Golfo Di Napoli (Bay of Naples) were very inviting indeed. I love fishing in a good depth close in as it provides the ideal circumstances for catching a variety of species. The first bout took place at Marina Grande, which was a tiny fishing hamlet towards one end of Sorrento. I chose to fish on a small jetty that gave me access to about 10 feet of clear water, as opposed to a shallower, rocky terrain on the quayside. The sea was very choppy which meant that I was unable to see any fish activity below the surface although I knew it would be teeming with life all the same. Experience had told me that to catch quickly I needed to fish with fine tackle so I selected a tiny pole float from my box and a size 20 hook to start. A single tentacle of the calamari was impaled on the hook and I set the float depth to about nine feet. The bait sank slowly but as soon as the float cocked, it bobbed under and I struck into the first fish that turned out to be a small Saddled Bream - a new species for me. This one was quickly followed by another first - a handsome Damsel Fish. Having caught early on in the session, I changed the tackle for the remaining 15 minutes or so to a leger rig and a size 12 hook baited with a nice strip of the white fleshy part of the squid. The change resulted in one bite and one lost fish that threw the hook as it surfaced. It looked like a Weever but I couldn't be sure - despite the lost fish it had been a good start to the campaign...

A couple of days later we had some free time so I packed the telescopic in the rucksack along with some ragworms purchased locally. On this occasion we ambled through the centre of Sorrento before making a detour towards the coast and the Marina Piccola. This was the main port of Sorrento where large jet boats ferry hundreds of visitors to the Island of Capri on a daily basis. Making our way to the end of the quay, passing long queues of people waiting to board the boats, we were stopped by one of the harbour officials who informed us that it was impossible to fish from the quay. This was a major disappointment to me because there was perhaps 30 or 40 feet of water here directly under the rod tip which was a mouth-watering prospect. However "Lady Luck" was with me on this occasion - just as we had retraced our steps to the harbour entrance, there was an announcement to the effect that sailings for the day had been postponed due to gale force winds. The place cleared within a few minutes and I was back in business again. A light paternoster leger rig was the order of the day to present the bait just off the bottom, alongside the quay wall. On the first drop down, the ragworm was intercepted by a Rainbow Wrasse, which I landed without any problem. A lean spell followed when I was unable to hit the finicky bites and I found myself continually reeling in the tackle unnecessarily to check the bait. During this period a nice sized fish with long barbels protruding from the underside of its mouth followed the bait up as I reeled in but turned away at the last minute when it saw me. I believe this colourful fish was a Red Mullet, although not having seen a live one before I couldn't be certain. Anyway, no more bites occurred on my next few drop downs and there was no sign of the fish following the bait up again so a slight change of tactics was necessary - more patience was called for to allow the tentative bites to develop further before striking. The next bite saw me connect with a good fish that needed to be played carefully on my 3lb main line. On the way up through the deep water my reel was conceding line with the jolting of the fish but gradually progress was made until I caught a glimpse of the Red Mullet approaching the surface. At that instant the hook link parted unexpectedly and the fish was lost. It was a shame and I could only think that the line must have come into contact with the concrete walling or the fish chafed the line with its mollusc devouring jaws. Either way it had gone and all I could do was continue fishing for the remaining few minutes to try and get another one of these strange looking fish. It wasn't to be though. My efforts were rewarded however, with three more fish including the rare capture of a Brown Comber. This little specimen which resembled a Perch was identified by its distinguishing black pelvic fins and the black smudge on its dorsal fin. I couldn't have asked for more and it certainly made up for the loss of the whiskered brute earlier. For the record the other fish taken were a White Sea Bream, which I had encountered previously in Corfu, and a second Rainbow Wrasse…

On the penultimate day of the holiday we paid a visit to the beautiful coastal village of Amalfi, situated on the fringes of the Bay of Salerno. Our journey took us on the scenic route that was very narrow and climbed in hairpin bends famous for the filming of the last scene of the classic 1960's movie, "The Italian Job". The experience of the spectacular views, sheer drops into deep blue sea and ooh's and aah's from the nervous coach passengers was worth every minute, and the fishing wasn't bad either! After looking around Amalfi I only had a 25-minute slot to fish so I needed to be on top of the game to be able to achieve something for the fishing record. Making my way to the end of the quay I looked down through the crystal clear water upon a bottom made up of large boulders. The depth was about 10 feet down the side of the wall and it quickly got deeper a few yards out. I could see a shoal of Damsel Fish but the Mullet were noticeably absent. My ploy was to flutter the bait across the boulders, utilising the tide pull with the aid of my tiny pole float. The hook was a size 14 and bait was a small strip of octopus that I had cadged from the kitchen staff at our hotel. First cast produced a Damsel Fish, which was taken on the drop, and the next a Saupe - a super looking fish and another new species. The Saupe is another member of the Sea Bream family, identified by the brown coloured horizontal lines traversing the flanks of the fish and its distinctive yellow eyes. After the early action, bites dried up fishing close in so I increased the float depth and cast further out into the deeper water. I was watching the carefully cut strip of pure white octopus flesh as it sank slowly through the clear water when suddenly it disappeared from view. My eyes turned instinctively to the float, which was just beginning to sail away and I struck into a nice fish. This one was obviously another type of Sea Bream although it differed from anything I had encountered to date. The mouth was comparatively large and angular and the scales of the fish were silvery and very small. It resembled a bright silver disc as it lay on my rag and when handling the fish it was smooth and soft to the touch. The fins were edged in black and uncharacteristically the dorsal was not spiky like most of its Sea Bream brethren. I took some photographs for the record and after returning home was able to make a positive identification - it was a junior Ray's Bream.

A Damsel Fish from the quay at Amalfi

I was very pleased with my results - five new species caught in less than two hours actual fishing overall. The deep waters of the area had lots of fishing potential and I would love to fish there again with proper tackle one day.

+++++

Epilogue

Here I am at the end of another angling era, which has seen mixed fortunes, and I'm now just about ready to begin the next phase – life goes on. My angling years are now far-reaching and I must admit that I am not finding it quite so easy to cope with the more extreme elements of my fishing, although my motivation remains as strong as ever. I am still mesmerised by water and like to be close to it, where I can scheme to my heart's content the downfall of my next adversary. My future plans have not yet been finalised but I would certainly like them to include some freshwater targets, like the Siamese Carp for instance. Now there's a glorious species, big and beautiful, but the quandary is that a marathon journey to Thailand might be necessary to bag one. My old chum Dave Wilson is living there now and I am sure that he will have caught a few and will be able to help me track one down – I must give him a ring sometime. If Asia doesn't transpire there's always Africa for a Tiger Fish and giant Nile Perch that inhabit that huge body of water known as Lake Nasser. As I dream on, I have always wanted to have a bash at ice fishing for Arctic Char and perhaps I can arrange a few days in Scandinavia if time permits. It's inconvenient and certainly a nuisance but work always seems to get in the way of my ambitions! Anyway, if I fail to take advantage of the aforementioned rather tough options, I could always take an easier route to locate a Large Mouth Bass, which seem to be far more widespread and obliging – ah well, I'll have to wait and see how things pan out.

Incidentally, one encouraging development since my previous book was published is that a team based at Brooksby Melton Fisheries College in Leicestershire is carrying out a scientific study which could pave way for the re-introduction of Burbot into Britain. Burbot make good eating and are in fact freshwater members of the Cod family and have been extinct in our waters for many years now. In order to carry out the necessary work, the team has brought back 42 specimens of varying weights up to 3lbs from the River Guden in Denmark. I sincerely hope that the study is a complete success as it could result in a re-stocking programme of this enigmatic species to be enjoyed by everyone. The thought of setting out to catch a Burbot in my own country is such a mouth-watering one for me that I hope the outcome is published without delay. I would like to think that my rantings on this subject in my last book (the chapter entitled "Going, Going, Gone") had some influence on this bold decision, as I find it difficult to believe that this is purely a coincidence.

Apart from the freshwater choices, there are a few salt-water species that I would dearly like to catch. However, these can be a little trickier to track down and catch because there are a lot of factors that can affect matters on the day. As an example, Cuckoo Wrasse is high on my list, but what is the ideal strategy for catching one of these? They prefer a rocky domain and relatively deep water so a boat is probably going to give the best chance of locating one. However, in practice, a boatman has a living to earn and is therefore unlikely to venture out to look for a solitary Cuckoo Wrasse when he can probably keep all his anglers happy by filling the fish-box with Bass or the like. Compound this little dilemma with the need to make sure that the weather and tide conditions are suitable, and the difficulty of the exercise begins to become clear. Of course there are the added complications of travel, which is likely to be 400 to 500 miles in round terms and the question of obtaining appropriate bait. I believe the problems can be overcome by talking to anglers in the know who can probably answer all the questions arising. One fellow who has been of great assistance to me is the famous and very approachable Mike Thrussell. Mike is a great all-round angler with a huge knowledge of a whole variety of sea fish. In fact he has passed on the locations of some of his special marks together with a number of tips to try my luck for various species including Sole, Smooth Hound and Trigger Fish. These are currently in the melting pot and I am looking forward to fitting them into my fishing schedule, so — watch this space!